your ORGANIC KITCHEN

+ The Essential Guide to +
Selecting and Cooking
Organic Foods

JESSE ZIFF COOL

Photography by Lisa Koenig

Front Cover and Recipe Photographer: Lisa Koenig
Individual Food Item Photography by Rodale Images
Cover and Interior Designer: Christina Gaugler
Cover Food Stylist: Nir Adar
Interior Food Stylist: Diane Simone Vezza
Prop Stylist: Janet Bowblis

The song lyrics on page 11 are from "Big Yellow Taxi" by Joni Mitchell. © 1970 Crazy Crow Music (Renewed). All rights administered by Sony/ATV Music Publishing, 8 Music Square West, Nashville, TN 37203. All rights reserved. Used by permission.

The recipe for Risotto D'Oro on page 64 is from *The Union Square Café Cookbook* by Danny Meyer. © 1994 by Danny Meyer and Michael Romano. Reprinted by permission of HarperCollins Publishers, Inc.

The recipe for Lamb Barbacoa on page 90 is reprinted with permission of Scribner, a division of Simon & Schuster, from *Mexican Kitchen* by Rick Bayless. © 1996 by Richard Lane Bayless.

The recipe for Avocado and Beet Salad with Citrus Vinaigrette on page 166 is from *Chez Panisse Café Cookbook* by Alice Waters. © 1999 by Alice Waters. Reprinted by permission of HarperCollins Publishers, Inc.

Library of Congress Cataloging-in-Publication Data

Cool, Jesse Ziff.
    Your organic kitchen : the essential guide to selecting and cooking organic foods /
    Jesse Ziff Cool ; photography by Lisa Koenig.
        p.   cm.
    Includes index.
    ISBN 1–57954–166–6 hardcover
    1. Cookery (Natural foods)   2. Natural foods.   I. Title.
    TX741 .C665   2000
    641.5'63—dc21   00–025488

Distributed to the book trade by St. Martin's Press

2 4 6 8 10 9 7 5 3 1 hardcover

Visit us on the Web at www.rodalecookbooks.com, or call us toll-free at (800) 848-4735.

Rodale would like to thank the following participating partners of *Your Organic Kitchen* for providing promotional consideration: *Cascadian Farm, Eden Foods, Horizon Organic Dairy*, and *Seeds of Change*.

RODALE

WE **INSPIRE** AND **ENABLE** PEOPLE TO IMPROVE
THEIR LIVES AND THE WORLD AROUND THEM

*T*his book is dedicated in gratitude to my organic-farmer friends, the men and women who choose hard work and meaningfulness as a way of life. They are my heroes, my mentors.

But it was my dear friend Stuart Dickson of Stone Free Farm who really taught me about organic farming. He made me get dirty, haul irrigation pipe, and plant endless rows of garlic. Every once in a while, for a moment in time, he actually let me pretend that I was really and truly a farm girl and not a restaurant owner.

In all Rodale cookbooks, our mission is to provide delicious and nutritious recipes. Our recipes also meet the standards of the Rodale Test Kitchen for dependability, ease, practicality, and, most of all, great taste. To give us your comments, call (800) 848-4735.

CONTENTS

INDIAN SUMMER *142*
A banquet of the harvest's bounty

AUTUMN HARVEST *172*
Colorful, flavorful, and quite memorable

EARLY WINTER *204*
A collection of rich and hearty flavors

DEEP OF WINTER *232*
Nourish the body and warm the soul

Mark Estes

ACKNOWLEDGMENTS

One does not write a book like this alone. I am humbly grateful to the team from Rodale for working with me and orchestrating all aspects of its personality.

But most of all, I thank Rodale for giving me Anne Egan, who is the editor from Heaven, full of patience, kindness, and compassion.

Recipes come alive through photographs. Thanks to photographer Lisa Koenig, food stylist Diane Vezza, prop stylist Janet Bowblis, and talented designer Christina Gaugler.

JoAnn Brader and the Test Kitchen staff at Rodale cooked and sampled each recipe and lifted my spirit via Anne through phone calls spilling over with compliments. Thank you to Nancy Zelko for gathering the facts to support my beliefs and Arden Moore for rounding out my words.

Merrilyn Lewis from Lisa Ekus Public Relations introduced me to the Rodale team. Yes, you were right, we were meant to make a beautiful book together.

Gene Kahn helped me clearly understand some intricate farming issues.

I am deeply grateful to Oldways Preservation and Trust and the Chef's Collaborative 2000 for supporting me and promoting healthful eating on so many levels. There are a handful of organizations that have brought organic farming to the forefront: Organic Farming Research Foundation, California Certified Organic Growers, and the Committee for Sustainable Agriculture. All are nonprofit organizations run by dedicated people who do their best to keep the old ways alive. They have nurtured me and encouraged me to keep believing that through our work, together and individually, we can change the world and make it a better place for our children.

I am always juggling a lot of projects, and in the midst of writing this book, I became a grandma (which is everything they say it is) and opened another restaurant. I am endlessly grateful to my staff for their support and patience. But most of all, I am grateful to Gustavo Caballero, who has for nearly 20 years worked at Flea St. Café, lovingly, respectfully, and loyally caring for both the restaurant and me. We have grown together, and there is a sweet magic to it all.

My family and friends (you know who you are) continue to tolerate the way I work and just keep loving and supporting me. Thank you, Brando, for daily words of affirmation. It came from the heart and meant so much.

MY ORGANIC ROOTS

I was a fortunate kid. My family's riches weren't measured in dollars but in the love that we felt and, in many ways, in the healthy foods that we ate. For the most part, our food was free of artificial flavors, preservatives, chemicals, and pesticides. My family wasn't on a deliberate organic crusade. We simply respected the old traditional ways of growing, gathering, and preparing foods in the healthiest and cleanest ways possible.

This philosophy of respecting and revering food goes back generations in my family—on both sides. I was blessed to have Jewish and Italian grandparents who loved to garden and cook. As a little girl growing up in a rural town near Pittsburgh, I remember helping my parents and grandparents tend their small backyard gardens. They taught me about living heirlooms—treasured seeds brought from the Old Country that they respectfully planted in American soil. They raised their own chickens, and my uncle Jack owned a slaughterhouse where naturally grazed cattle were processed and aged properly.

Cooking and the dinner table were always at the heart of our household. Being Jewish and Italian meant endless conversations about both food and life itself. Because of this rich ethnic mix, our months were filled with celebrations. These featured bounties of food, tables loaded with delicious

dishes, and homes filled with laughing, loving family and friends. Bottles of cooking wine and olive oil were always present. Plates were always piled with greens, both fresh and steamed. Garlic was as common a condiment as salt and pepper. Onions seemed to find their way into nearly every dish.

My grandmother Edna was a remarkable cook. She taught me how to make ravioli and other dishes from scratch. She got the meat from Uncle Jack, roasted it, and cooked it for what seemed like an eternity. While the meat slowly simmered, she went to work making homemade pasta. My two brothers would be outside playing, while I would happily be by my nana's side in the kitchen learning how to make ravioli, polenta, and platters full of slow-cooked meats and vegetables. This was my idea of playtime well-spent. I can almost smell the inviting aromas of those memories. To this day, cooking and eating good foods are at the heart and soul of my existence.

I still chuckle recalling all those times when Papa, my Italian grandfather, cajoled me into accompanying him on his "special missions" to pluck wild dandelions and onions from yards all over the neighborhood. We would rush home, rinse the leaves, season them with a little olive oil, salt, and pepper, and enjoy our green treat.

My parents, Eddie and June, continued this organic-food tradition. My mom was the family nurturer, always there with soft, gentle hugs. Back then and still today, she trusts in me and encourages me to pursue my dreams and never sacrifice my integrity as an owner of an organic restaurant. My dad is an enthusiastic lover of the Earth. Now 83, he gardened with passion, passing along the joy of watching something grow and then paying homage to it when it reached the table.

I also remember those early Saturday mornings, hearing the sounds of a truck pulling into our driveway with yet another load of organic material for our garden. Dad inspired me with his love for growing plants. He relied on natural remedies to solve pest problems without the need for pesticides and was rewarded with the neighborhood's juiciest and biggest tomatoes. His garden stretched everywhere in the yard, including between the shrubbery, where he planted melons and cucumbers.

The Ageless Value of Food

Natural food remedies were a part of my family's medicine chest. Garlic and onions were used in food dishes as well as in herbal medicines to fight off colds and fevers. I was taught that eating the right foods keeps you healthy. It's just that simple. I believe in that. In general, most of us don't take vitamins. We don't see the need. We get all our nutrients from a well-balanced diet including lots of organic foods that we eat every day.

I see the living proof in following this philosophy every time I look at my parents. My mom is going strong at 80. My dad is a vibrant 83-year-old still selling organic produce for Stone Free Farm at the local farmers' market. To this day, he tucks a fresh green sprig behind his ear for good luck. My parents still cook from scratch, creatively making use of the bounty that my dad gathers at the market. I equate their long lives and young attitudes with the wholesome food that they have always eaten—that, and their lasting love for each other.

Decades have passed since my childhood. Now, I am a mother of two sons, and I'm a new grandmother. Just like my grandparents and parents, I too am passing on the family tradition of supporting organic gardening and cooking.

It hasn't been easy convincing my sons at times. My older son, Joshua, still jokes about what it was like to have a mom who was a hippie. At school, no one would trade lunches with him. Joshua complained that compared with the processed foods of his peers, his lunches tasted like dry canned food on sandpaper bread. He grew up during the time before the supply of good-tasting organic meats and products was readily available.

At school barbecues, he was the only student stepping up to the grill with tofu and veggie hot dogs. He grew up thinking that crackers were cookies—until he got to school and learned the truth. Later, as most teens tend to do, he rebelled and turned into a junk-food junkie. He nicknamed me Granola Head and Earth Hugger.

Now, as a new father, Joshua and his wife, Yuko, understand why I insisted on feeding him organic foods. It was done out of love and concern for his health. Determined to keep his son, Zachary, healthy, Joshua is careful about the baby foods he provides.

Jonah, my younger son, embraced the organic philosophy more easily. His only major act of rebellion centered on organic milk. He hated the taste. I bought organic milk that was pasteurized but not homogenized. It came in glass bottles, so you could see the cream at the top. To me, there were two benefits: The glass bottle was returnable, and the milk was delicious and real. That didn't matter to Jonah. He would sneak to the neighbor's house and trade our milk for their milk that came out of plastic gallon jugs. The neighbors loved it. I didn't know what to do. Now, however, he enjoys homogenized organic milk.

I occasionally let him "junk out" on processed foods, while trying to gently enlighten him about the benefits of fresh foods. Now a young adult, Jonah prefers to eat organic foods and makes very wise food choices.

My kitchen is known among Jonah's high school buddies as the place for the best-tasting after-school snacks. The refrigerator is often filled with homemade pastas, soups, and healthy munchies. No artificial ingredients or chemicals are in any of the foods that I prepare. It is real food cooked by a real person, and there is usually plenty of it.

They look out the back door and are no longer surprised to see my chickens clucking about in the middle of suburban Palo Alto, California. I want my sons and their friends to taste healthy, real eggs from chickens that are fed organic food. I want them to see how excited I get when I cut up freshly picked organic string beans, tomatoes, celery, and onions from my funky little garden and prepare a dish. It is important to me that they see me put on my "farmer girl" boots, dig in the dirt, and feed the chickens.

I share these stories as a parent to let you know how important it is to practice what you believe. And trust that in time, your children will see the love and commitment behind your decision to eat organic foods whenever given the choice.

At the same time, I accept that my children and I are a part of the real world. We need to do our best to live honorably and respectfully on the planet. My goal as a parent has always been to just make them conscious of what they eat.

During a speaking engagement, I told the audience that when I die, I want my children and their children to have clear visions of my refrigerator full of home-cooked foods made from organic ingredients. Even in the midst of their busy and hectic lives, I want them to maintain that vision of me standing at the prep table cooking with love for them.

A Lifelong Love of Cooking

By now, it's easy to see how I see myself: I am a cook. A very happy one. Always have been and always will be a cook. Feeding others makes me happy. So does being treated to a special meal prepared by a loved one. Naturally, I prefer the ingredients to be organic, but I take more joy in knowing that someone has taken the time to cook for me. The spirit in which a dish is prepared is often as nurturing as the food itself.

I grew up during the 1950s, a decade characterized by the emergence of convenient, processed foods. Even my family was seduced at times by the allure of fast foods and convenient processed foods. A lunchtime sandwich often consisted of a freshly picked organic tomato and a handful of lettuce from my dad's garden slathered with Miracle Whip on two slices of Wonder Bread.

This explains my realistic view of organics. I am conscious of and careful about what I eat. There are times when there is nothing better than a corned beef and chopped liver sandwich at a Jewish deli. Still, my pantry is predominantly organic and free of artificial ingredients and chemicals. My restaurant features about 95 percent organic ingredients on the menu. I walk the walk, but I am not ashamed to occasionally wander off the path.

Giving Back to the Community

I give credit to my parents for my business success. Each of them contributed in different ways.

During my childhood, Dad reigned as King Eddie, owner of King Edward's Supermarket. He ran his store with respect and integrity for his customers and employees. He would wow customers with his array of organic meats and produce. His bakers never used prepared mixes, making fruit pies, whole grain breads, and even doughnuts from scratch. My dad delighted in creating custard from real milk and churning gallons of strawberry and peach ice cream made with real fruit, usually organic, grown on local farms. By age 12, I was working side by side with him and loving every minute.

My dad taught me what it meant to be a part of the community. He often organized benefits to help those in need. For me, even during lean times in the restaurant when my staff would urge me to cut back on costs, I tried to maintain my level of charity and civic work. There were times when things got tough, and it was my mother who supported my bottom line: the use of organic products over making lots of money.

At the age of 27, with my first husband and a buddy of his, I opened my first organic restaurant. At that time, there were no organic restaurants, so buying enough organic foods was challenging. Still, I was determined to serve food that was healthy for people and the environment. After a long search, I finally found a local produce company that delivered organic foods. It was called the *3:30 A.M. Produce Company*, and it was run by two wonderful, dynamic, high-spirited women. We would also hit the farmers' market every Saturday to buy produce.

I was told over and over again that using organic ingredients in a restaurant was not realistic from a cost perspective. Granted, I may not have made as much profit as others, but after 25 years in the restaurant business, I feel incredibly successful. One of the keys to the success of using organic foods is to run a seasonal menu. Seasonal fresh foods tend to be less expensive, and the flavors are deep and genuine.

Every day, I feel profoundly grateful to everyone who has been patient and supportive of my efforts—my family, my staff, my customers. As you can see, food was and remains the heart of my soul. As a daughter, a mother, a grandmother, and a business owner, I maintain my unwavering commitment to using organic foods as often as possible. To me, restaurants as well as home kitchens should be places where food is simply as pure as it can be, and always served with love.

WHY ORGANIC?

or•gan•ic \or-'ga-nik\ *adj*: of, relating to, yielding, or involving the use of food produced with the use of feed or fertilizer of plant or animal origin without employment of chemically formulated fertilizers, growth stimulants, antibiotics, or pesticides

Let's consider what our great-grandparents grew up eating. Most likely, they enjoyed vine-ripened tomatoes and juicy red strawberries grown in nutrient-rich soil, pampered with fresh spring water, and warmed by sunshine. Most likely, the fruits and vegetables came from a nearby farm and were grown by a farmer everyone knew by his first name.

Our ancestors grew up in a time when "fresh," "natural," and "organic" foods went without saying and without the need for any special labeling.

The primary food additives were preservatives and seasonings like vinegar and salt, not difficult-to-pronounce, strange-sounding chemicals like monosodium glutamate. Our great-grandmothers planned and adjusted their meals around foods of the season, and they hunkered down for long winters by relying on the local produce that they had canned and preserved in the previous summer and autumn.

The fruits and vegetables they ate were naturally grown, unadulterated organic foods. But the term *organic* was never mentioned. For them, food was fresh, celebrated, and most of all, safe.

Today, many of us health-conscious eaters desire, even demand, that foods from supermarkets and restaurants be as good and pure as foods enjoyed by families who lived three generations ago. Our voices are being heard.

Look around you. Signs of this retro food evolution are everywhere. Even as recently as the 1980s, supermarkets separated tomatoes strictly by type—plum or beefsteak, for instance. Now, they are distinguished by variety, color, and how they are grown.

Instead of being grown for flavor and ripened by the sun, the majority of supermarket tomatoes usually spend their infancy inside huge greenhouses. They are nursed with synthetic fertilizers and engineered for shelf life and visual appeal. After their stay in the greenhouse, they are transplanted to mile-stretching fields saturated with 400 to 600 pounds per acre of more fertilizer and fumigated with methyl bromide, a weed-killing toxic gas. Weekly, crop planes unleash fungicides and insecticides that destroy plant pests and diseases—and, unfortunately, some migrating birds. But the public has been led to believe that they are the best kind of tomatoes because they are uniform and perfect-looking.

Today, in many stores, there are more choices. Look for the smaller tomato section, the one that is vibrant with a vast array of colors and shapes and, yes, the one that typically costs a little more per pound. There is a good chance that you will spot the "certified organic" label— a signal to health-conscious shoppers that each and every one of these red, gold, purple, and green beauties enjoyed a splendid beginning. They developed from seeds that inherently have unique flavors, have not been genetically modified, and are grown in nutrient-rich soil on small, local organic farms free of artificial chemicals, pesticides, and commercial fertilizers.

This organic return stretches beyond your local supermarket. Many restaurant owners now proudly highlight their menus with organically prepared dishes, showcasing the farms' names and indicating their preference for organically raised foods.

History of Organic Farming

*W*ho should we thank for starting the organic food movement? Perhaps the better question is, who rescued it and brought it back? Before 1900, all food was organically grown. Of course, farmers and shoppers didn't call it by that phrase. They didn't need to. They knew that what they ate came from a local farmer they probably knew, who had grown it with care, love, and purity. There was no need to be concerned about safety or pollution.

Then the age of mass production arrived, intermingled with a couple of world wars. America had many more mouths to feed. We needed to grow lots of food in a hurry. Scientists discovered that chemicals sprayed on crops could kill pests and plant diseases instantly. They also developed artificial flavorings to perk up people's palates and preservatives to make foods last longer and maintain an eye-catching

appearance. Produce grown in south Florida began being loaded into large trucks and train cars to be delivered 3,000 miles away to supermarkets all over the country.

In our haste to produce foods more quickly, a few visionaries began questioning the price that our bodies and our planet were sacrificing for this technology. Sir Albert Howard, a British agricultural scientist, was the first to consciously reject modern "agri-chemical" methods back in the 1930s. He argued that artificial fertilizers and poisonous insecticides had no place in farming. He figured out a way to turn town wastes—animal manure, compost, grass turf, and straw—into usable nutrient materials that were tilled into the soil to nourish plants in a safe way. He called this nutrient recycling system the Wheel of Life.

Here in the United States, J. I. Rodale embraced Sir Albert's views. It was Rodale who in 1940 popularized the term *organic*. Rodale left New York City and purchased a 65-acre farm in rural eastern Pennsylvania. He grew all his crops without chemical fertilizers or pesticides. Rodale strongly believed that healthy soil produces healthy foods, which in turn, help keep people healthy. He began sharing his philosophy in 1942, when he founded *Organic Gardening* magazine, a publication now being continued by his grandchildren. He remains one of my first heroes in the organic farming movement.

Even back in the 1940s, Rodale warned that using pesticides and artificial fertilizers would pollute our farmlands, lakes, rivers, and air. An excerpt from his book *Pay Dirt* reads:

"People felt they could afford—with a continent to develop—to wear out a farm and move to another. That day has passed. Badly eroded, worn-out soil will not recover overnight, but fertility can be restored. Land still fertile can be kept so, with composts, and be constantly improved."

There are many modern-day heroes carrying forth these beliefs. They range from the founders of organic food companies to the small local farmers doing their bit one acre at a time. Behind the scenes are researchers studying the health advantages of organic foods and many nonprofit organizations supporting the environment and sustainable politics. I salute all those working for this great goal.

Health Reasons to Choose Organic

Remember all those times your mom said, "Drink your milk!" and "Eat your fruits and vegetables. They're good for you!"? Many of us growing up in the 1950s, 1960s, and 1970s scoffed at that message. Hamburgers, french fries, and chocolate malts tasted so much better.

But Mom was right. Nutritionists and doctors, backed by scientific evidence, continue telling us that fresh fruits and vegetables are loaded with essential vitamins and minerals that we need to keep our bodies healthy. Doesn't it make sense that the foods we eat and the nutrients they contain would effect the functioning of our bodies? We now know that blueberries, for instance, contain antioxidants, known to fight off cancer-causing free radical molecules. Broccoli and milk are loaded with calcium, which we need to maintain strong bones. And this is just the beginning.

Rather than just hearing that real food is good for us, we are learning how and why it is life-supportive. I remember when I was invited to speak about organic cooking to physicians and medical students at Stanford University School of Medicine a few years back. After serving them a luscious and beautiful lunch made with all organic ingredients, I asked them how they felt. Many responded with one word: "Great!" I then asked them to think of their bodies as they might their cars. "Many of you will someday drive a Porsche, BMW, or Mercedes," I said, "and I doubt if you would even think of putting cheap fuel into the tanks of your cars. Think, then, of food as our fuel. Eat the best foods, and your body will run smoothly."

Throughout the 1990s, the healthy message campaign nudged us a little toward eating better, but the real push, what really brought it to the forefront, was the issue of food safety. Remember the milk scare in the 1990s? Is it any wonder that many people, even those who are not committed to the organic food movement, still avoid cow's milk? The public responded to the fact that some commercial farmers injected their cows with a genetically engineered hormone called recombinant bovine growth hormone (rBGH). Some researchers saw a possible link between rBGH and certain cancers such as breast and prostate. Organic farmers never give their cows growth hormones or antibiotics, so all their milk, cheese, and other dairy products are free from these substances. The cows are given a wholesome diet of organic grains and feed.

Large amounts of pesticides have been found in what would otherwise be considered wholesome foods. Unfortunately, if you eat out-of-season foods not grown organically, which are shipped from all corners of the planet, there is a good chance that they are tainted with ripening agents and pesticides. Conventionally grown apples, for example, are typically sprayed with 32 different pesticides. During winter months, it is not unusual to see New Zealand strawberries, Mexican tomatoes, or Chilean grapes. Researchers at the Rodale Institute in Kutztown, Pennsylvania, determined that a large portion of the fresh food that we eat daily travels an average of 1,400 miles from the farm to our plates.

These "food miles" come at a cost to our health. Nonorganic Chilean grapes, for instance, represent 90 percent of all winter grapes consumed by Americans. Yet they rank among the top foods contaminated with toxic pesticide residues. This scares me.

We need fruits, vegetables, and milk to sustain us and keep our immune systems strong enough to fend off invading viruses and bacteria. So what should we do? Keep eating plenty of fresh fruits and vegetables. Do not avoid dairy products, meats, or fish. The solution is to be more selective. When given a choice, opt for certified organic

THE TOP 10 FOODS TO EAT ORGANICALLY

Some conventionally grown foods are treated with more pesticides than others. Some retain more of the pesticides. Here is a list of the top 10 foods containing the most pesticides, according to the Environmental Working Group, a nonprofit research group based in Washington, D.C.

You can sidestep harm and still eat vitamin-rich foods. If you cannot find these foods organically, here are some great alternatives that contain the same valuable vitamins and minerals.

High-Pesticide Food	Main Nutrient	Healthy Alternatives
Strawberries	Vitamin C	Blueberries, raspberries, oranges, grapefruit, kiwifruit, watermelon
Bell peppers	Vitamin C	Green peas, broccoli, romaine lettuce
Spinach	Vitamins A and C	Broccoli, Brussels sprouts, asparagus
Cherries	Vitamin C	Oranges, blueberries, raspberries, kiwifruit, blackberries, grapefruit
Peaches	Vitamins A and C	Nectarines, watermelon, tangerines, oranges, grapefruit
Mexican cantaloupe	Vitamins A and C and potassium	U.S. cantaloupe grown from May to December, watermelon
Celery	Carotenoids	Carrots, broccoli, radishes, romaine lettuce
Apples	Vitamin C	Watermelon, nectarines, bananas, tangerines
Apricots	Vitamins A and C and potassium	Nectarines, watermelon, oranges, tangerines
Green beans	Potassium	Green peas, broccoli, cauliflower, Brussels sprouts, potatoes, asparagus

produce at supermarkets, natural food stores, food cooperatives, farmers' markets, or local farm stands. Buy from and regularly support farmers who you know practice organic cultivation, even if they are not certified.

There will be times when organic foods are not readily available. When you need to buy conventionally grown fruits and vegetables, make it a habit to thoroughly scrub them under running water to remove traces of chemicals from their skins and crevices.

As for dairy products, I choose only organic products, which are readily available in most supermarkets. To me, it's a safer choice. Others agree. Since the mid-1990s, when rBGH news made headlines, sales of organic milk have increased by leaps and bounds.

Environmental Reasons to Choose Organic

A lot has changed during my time on this planet. Beautiful unspoiled meadows that I remember as a little girl are paved over with strip malls. Trout-filled streams and lakes now display "off-limits" signs due to pollution. The crystal blue, seemingly invincible sky that I marveled at as a child succumbs a bit more each year to smog and the diminishing ozone layer. As Joni Mitchell sang, "Don't it always seem to go, that you don't know what you've got till it's gone? They paved paradise and put up a parking lot."

It's easy to blame vehicle exhaust fumes and industrial waste for the tainting of our land, waters, and sky. Yes, they've made an impact. But you may be surprised to learn that agriculture is the biggest polluter. The Environmental Protection Agency has proven that agriculture has polluted one-fourth of all American rivers and streams. American farmers are spraying pesticides at a rate five times more than they did in the 1960s.

Each one of us can contribute to cleaning our air, land, and water by making conscious choices each time we shop, prepare meals, and take out the trash. My heroes remain the growing legend of organic farmers—environmental pioneers—who with commitment and vision have chosen the old way, opting for compost and other natural fertilizers to create healthy soils that yield healthy plants. Using integrated pest management, they control pests with beneficial insects, not pesticides. They rotate crops to maintain the soil's fertility. They provide certified organic feed to their cows and chickens.

These farmers are doing their part to protect our soil, our water, and our air. They recognize the dramatic impact that a single commodity—food—makes on our environment. They are forming alliances and working together for the betterment of all.

I believe that we must support the preservation of farmland, but I hope that someday, organic farmers will grow all the food that we eat. In my restaurant, we try to do our part to protect the environment. I use menus made from recycled paper and nontoxic ink. We use containers made from recycled materials that are also recyclable. At my newest restaurant, *jZcool eatery and catering company* in Menlo Park, California, I began offering patrons the option for returnable glass plates for takeout foods. They pay a small deposit and return the plates. With all the takeout food eaten these days, it is our responsibility to limit our deposits to the mounting landfills.

The Importance of Flavor

As a restaurant owner and food lover, I believe that flavor is another important reason to choose organic products. Most often, they have more flavor than their conventional counterparts. This great taste is the reason why many chefs—even those not active in the organic movement—are purchasing organic products. A survey conducted by the National Restaurant Association found that 50 percent of restaurants with per-person dinner checks of $25 or more are now offering organic items on their menus.

I suggest that you test these preferences for yourself. Taste test the organic items available on your market's shelves, and you too will be a believer. The depth of genuine flavor will convince you that not only are organic products better for you and the environment but they are so much more delicious.

Why Pay More— Willingly?

Cost. This remains a major issue among newcomers to the organic world. Yes, organic products can cost more in terms of dollars and cents. But you reap the dividends in having a healthier body and knowing that you are promoting sustainable, healthy farms and not harming the environment.

There are still bargains to be found. Organic foods in season may sometimes cost less than foods shipped over long distances. The locally grown foods don't have far to travel and so do not incur transportation costs.

Consider these factors, and you will see the true value of buying organic.

🫐 Organic farms are more often labor-intensive in soil preparation, planting, weeding, and harvesting. The costs of weed control are much higher on organic farms.

🫐 Most organic farmers practice crop rotation, which costs more than planting the same crop season after season in the same location. The advantage of crop rotation is that disease, weed, and insect cycles are interrupted through the rotation process. Nature harbors simplicity. The complexity created by rotating crops aids in the control of farm pests.

🫐 Natural pesticides and integrated pest management can be more expensive than pesticides and insecticides and in general, are far less intrusive on the environment.

🫐 Organic feed for livestock costs more than conventional feed, but you are assured that the livestock are not consuming harmful chemicals that could be passed on to you.

🫐 Organic crops are frequently harvested at the peak of flavor, so they may have a shorter shelf life.

🫐 Organic companies often have to spend more money to use recycled paper, plastic, and other materials that decompose in the country's landfills.

Sustainable Cuisine

You may begin hearing the term *sustainable cuisine*. It was conceived by a group of America's most influential and well-known chefs who belong to a nonprofit organization called the Chefs Collaborative 2000. The concept of sustainable cuisine embraces the full cycle of what it means to cook, eat, and integrate organic foods into our everyday lives in a responsible way.

Many who practice sustainable cuisine use locally produced ingredients and organic foods and support composting as well as responsible fishing, farming, and meat production. Recycling and using nonharmful chemicals for cleaning and packaging are also goals. By showing concern, chefs and restaurant owners become accountable for their role in the well-being of people and of this planet.

Mindful Eating

We live in a hectic, fast-paced world with many—sometimes too many—choices. By creating an organic kitchen, you play a small but vital part in supporting the ethics of sustainable cuisine. When it comes to shopping, gardening, cooking, and eating, you can make your choices with deliberate consciousness. At the same time, I believe this should be done with joyfulness. If you spend too much time fretting over foods or worrying if you are making the right choices, the sensuality and the beauty of food can be easily forgotten.

Recognize that you won't always have access to organic products. Be kind to yourself when you answer the urge for junk food and indulge in something that might be considered unhealthy. I admit that whenever I go to a baseball game, I eat a hot dog loaded with mustard, onions, and relish. I don't chastise myself, because I know that human beings are not perfect and that these urges are natural. These indulgences are fine if they are occasional and not a part of our daily lives.

Whenever I travel or stay with friends, I try not to push the organic issue. Years ago, I was adamant until my older son, Josh, pointed out to me that, at times, I was self-righteous and overzealous. Believing in the benefits of using organic, clean foods doesn't mean that we have the right to impose it on others. This approach rarely works anyway. It is better to lead through example.

I've spent my lifetime trying to eat right and prepare the best possible foods for my family, my friends, and my restaurant patrons. I continue to applaud and support organic farmers who commit to growing the healthiest and, in my opinion, the best-tasting food in the world.

You, too, have a wonderful opportunity to save the environment and preserve the health of your family. It all starts with a shopping cart.

YOUR ORGANIC PANTRY

Now that you've made the decision to convert your kitchen to an organic one, recognize that this can't be done overnight. Pace yourself and celebrate every step along the way. This is a time of tiny triumphs. Little by little, day by day, week by week, add more organic ingredients into your existing kitchen. Forget the past and don't fret about what you haven't done or can't do. Embrace this transformation as a rebirth, a fresh start in creating a healthy you. Then take a step back and acknowledge all the reasons that prompted you into making this life-turning decision: You want to prepare the healthiest and safest foods available for your family and yourself. You want to do your part to protect the environment. You want to show your support for local organic farmers. Along the way, you will evolve into a compassionate consumer as you consciously make the choice to select foods nurtured in healthy soil and free of pesticides and other harmful contaminates.

The best place to start is in your own kitchen. Peruse your shelves for common ingredients that you use on a regular basis. Make a list of these ingredients. Move on to the refrigerator. You may also want to look through your recipe box for family favorites and the main ingredients in them. Complete your list, then it's time to go shopping.

Many supermarkets now carry an abundance of organic products. There are even some large natural supermarkets that carry the greatest percentage of organic products. Don't worry if neither of these options is available to you. Natural-food stores do carry many organic products, and there is also a growing number of mail-order options available. (Be sure to check the resource guide on page 261.)

Start by familiarizing yourself with the organic areas of the market. I have seen supermarkets that have one large section dedicated to organic products. Others have one small organic area in each aisle, and still others simply scatter organic products in among conventionally produced items. Take the time to walk through the store and look for all the organic products available. If you have the inclination, ask the store manager to direct you to the organic sections and thank him for providing them. Encourage him to stock more organic products and be sure to buy them. The more organic products you buy, the more the stores will carry.

With your list in hand, start filling your cart with the many organic products available. Remember, this can be a slow process. You may want to pick up just a few new items a week. When it comes to prepared foods, you will be able to easily stock your cupboards with organic broths, soups, grain mixes, canned beans, nut butters, tomato products, salad dressings, cookies, dips, and chips, to name just a few.

Depending on your store's selection, locating fresh produce can often be a bit more challenging. Besides supermarkets and natural-food stores, don't forget about the farmers in your area. Your best bet is to start at your local roadside farm stand or farmers' market. Sometimes, especially when you're buying from small local farms, the products may not always be certified organic, even if their growing practices are. It takes a minimum of 3 years and the passing of stringent requirements to earn this distinction. During this process of becoming organic, these farms are classified as transitional, which means that they are participating in the clean farming methods of certified organic farms. I buy as many certified organic products as I can, but I also buy from transitional producers.

Some small farms may not have had the time to do all the paperwork to become certified, but they may still be practicing organic methods, so be sure to ask. Talk to them about their growing methods, buy their products, and encourage them to become certified. When possible, visiting the farm or place of production is a good way of seeing firsthand how a product is developed.

Many communities now have farms or groups of farms called Community Supported Agriculture, or CSA. These are an ideal way to buy seasonal organic produce. CSA farms fill boxes or bags with whatever is growing locally and seasonally. You often don't know what will be in

Where to Begin

READING THE LABELS

Without question, the surest way to determine if food is organic is to look for a symbol of certification from either a state or a private organization. At farmers' markets, they are prominently displayed at the organic farm stands. On processed foods, these symbols are also displayed on the label or package, often on the front, so that you will know immediately that it is certified organic.

But let the buyer beware! Just as the word *lite* is used as a marketing tool (it doesn't necessarily mean that a food contains less fat), a label with just the word *organic* does not guarantee that the food is indeed free of pesticides. Many of us already read labels for calories and fat content. Apply those same scrutinizing skills in your search for authentic organic products. Look for a certified organic seal on the package. And as you scan the ingredient list, look to see that the ingredients listed are organic.

the box from week to week. Half of the fun is anticipating what will be in your next delivery. You might also get items that you wouldn't even consider buying. Celebrate this opportunity to experience new foods.

Purchasing organic meats, poultry, dairy products, and fish can be a bit more confusing. Here's some basic information to help you.

Meat. Fortunately (and finally), organic certification standards exist for meat products. For farmers to earn this standard, their animals must graze on organic fields and eat all-organic diets. The animals are free of any growth hormones or unnecessary antibiotics. Look for products with the organic certification seal. If these aren't available, your next best choice is to find meats that are ethically raised and free of growth hormones and antibiotics. This information is prominently displayed on the package. Speak to the butcher in your market and ask how the meat is raised and processed.

Poultry. Whenever possible, buy organically raised chicken or turkey. These birds have been raised on organic grains and feed and are free of growth hormones and unnecessary antibiotics. Fresh chicken and turkey are ideal, but if you live in a location where only frozen is available, that's a good option. Free-range chicken and turkey are often considered more healthy. However, the designation "free-range" means only that the bird spends a minimum of 2½ hours a day out of its pen. It does not guarantee that it is organically raised. So be sure to purchase organic poultry.

Seafood. Unfortunately, there is no certification for organic fish yet. Until that occurs, I recommend that you use locally caught fish and seafood whenever possible. I say this with a note of caution. Learn about the environment where the fish and seafood come from. Make sure it comes from clean, healthy water. Eating fish as soon as possible after it is caught or harvested is best. Sometimes, that means using fish that has been frozen immediately after being caught. Wild fish is also healthy if it's from clean waters such as those in Alaska. With the dwindling number of wild fish in our waters and shifts in sea temperatures, however, you may be selecting fish raised in fish farms. Ask questions. Using farm-raised fish is a healthy option only if you are satisfied with how the fish are raised, fed (on organic foods and without antibiotics), and handled after harvesting.

Wild game. Wild game is just that: caught in the wild. These animals live and feed naturally off the environment. This doesn't necessarily mean that their meat is organic, but the animals will not have received antibiotics or growth hormones. Depending on where they grazed, they may be as clean as organic animals, so wild game is a good choice.

Eggs. In your quest for organic eggs, remember that the egg comes from the chicken. So if you want organic eggs, it simply means that they'll come from organically raised chickens. The color of eggs is determined by the variety of the chicken, nothing more. So again, select eggs that have earned organic certification.

Dairy. Organic milks are readily available. If your market does not carry organic milk, request that they do. The cows, goats, and sheep that produce organic milk graze on organic grasses and are never given growth hormones or antibiotics. There are many other organic dairy products available as well. Look for butter, sour cream, yogurt, and cheeses.

Make shopping for organic foods a new and fun experience. Remember to take your time and try various products until you find the perfect ones for your table. And, no matter where you live, take into consideration that it is unlikely that you'll have access to every organic ingredient during all times of the year. Pace yourself and enjoy the process. Over time, your pantry will be a healthy organic one.

EDEN FOODS

Eden® Foods was founded on the simple principles of macrobiotics, as introduced to the West by the late George Ohsawa. By returning to a more peaceful way of growing, handling, and enjoying food, the founders believed that peace on Earth could ultimately be achieved. Today, more than 30 years later, this remains Eden's dream and mission.

In the late 1960s, organic farming on a commercial scale was practically unheard of. In the beginning, those at Eden traveled the back roads through the rolling farmland of south central Michigan, asking farmers if they were willing to grow foods without petrochemical pesticides or fertilizers. Some were inspired, as was Eden, by visionaries like Ohsawa, Rachel Carson, and J. I. Rodale. Many wanted to bring life back to their soil. When Eden offered these farmers a fair and premium price for their future organic crops, some were willing to try.

Eden's dedicated network of organic growers and suppliers quickly grew as they began to procure safer, more nourishing foods. Gradually, Eden has seen, year by year, their foods become more nutritious and delicious.

In 1972, Eden expanded into its first warehouse and established direct relations with the most highly respected makers of Japanese traditional and macrobiotic foods. Through the years, Eden has continued to nurture relationships with organic growers and traditional food makers throughout the United States, Canada, and beyond.

In 1983, Edensoy®, the first soymilk cooked properly for people, was introduced. Edensoy virtually created the nondairy liquid food category with its phenomenal acceptance and customer satisfaction. Eden's processing facilities are certified organic and circle-K kosher. Each step in the growing and handling of Eden brand foods is taken with great care.

In the mid-1970s, Eden played a key role in developing the organic certification pro-

Courtesy of Eden Foods

Eden helps to support 30,000 acres of organic, family farmland.

cesses used today and drafted the first American standards for "field to shelf" organic food production. Eden works with a select group of organic certifiers who insist upon an audit trail, which is deemed essential before calling a food organic. Eden was the first food manufacturer to speak out against irradiation, genetically engineered organisms (GEOs), and the threat to organic standards under the USDA. Today, the company is pioneering the due diligence system to assure that its food is not contaminated with untested genetically engineered experiments.

Over the past decade, organic food has become a multibillion-dollar industry that is marked by mergers, public stock offerings, and acquisitions of organic food companies by conventional food

Vital soil and good food are the keys to a healthy future on Earth.

manufacturers. Many companies have been observed taking every conceivable shortcut in order to cash in. "Conversely, Eden has remained independent and true to our founding principles and goals, 'Creation and Maintenance of Purity in Food™,'" says company president Michael J. Potter.

The proof is in the soymilk. In 1997, the *New York Times* tested for the presence of GEOs in 11 soy- and corn-based foods, and the only one that tested negative was Edensoy. Eden patrons know and appreciate the diligence, effort, and resources required to provide the country's finest food.

"We are blessed with dedicated growers, employees, business partners, and associates who share our goals," says Potter, "and we are gratified to work with 350 organic family farms, supporting more than 30,000 acres of vibrant organic soil—teeming with living ecosystems."

FIRST OF SPRING

By the time winter nears its end, I am ready, waiting, and hungry for the treasures of spring to shoot up from the moist, cool soil. The spring rains, interrupted only by glimpses of sunshine, yield tender yet full-flavored greens, tiny sweet lettuces, pea shoots, asparagus, artichokes, and wild mushrooms. Sugar snap peas and spring onions follow, inspiring the creation of lighter dishes from my organic kitchen.

Asparagus remains the star, and for good reason. There are few vegetables that rival its popularity and versatility at this time of the year. Whether they're steamed and eaten chilled with a garlicky dip, tossed in salads, pureed into soups, grilled on the barbecue, or wrapped in salty meats, many of us just can't seem to get enough of these tender spears.

Next on my springtime prized list is the artichoke. I remember the days when it was next to impossible to find organic artichokes. To satisfy our cravings, my son Jonah and I would treat ourselves to nonorganic artichokes. We regarded them as our "must-have junk food." These days, more artichokes are grown organically, so we eat them often.

Early spring is a time that beckons me back to the farmers' market after a long, dormant winter. I relish this time and urge you to seek out and gather information from farmers, fishermen, ranchers, cheese makers, bread bakers and, most important, people in charge of every department in your local grocery store.

KITCHEN TIP

This recipe is quite flexible. Try using sweet potatoes instead of the white, and fresh or frozen peas in the place of the sugar snap peas.

SUGAR SNAP PEA AND POTATO CAKES

10	sugar snap peas, trimmed
4	tablespoons olive oil
1	large onion, thinly sliced
2	garlic cloves, minced
2	cups cooked mashed potatoes
1	cup (4 ounces) shredded Cheddar cheese
3	tablespoons unbleached all-purpose flour
½	teaspoon salt
¼	teaspoon freshly ground black pepper
4	cups mesclun or spring salad mix
1	large carrot, peeled into curls

Bring a small saucepan of water to a boil over high heat. Add the snap peas and blanch in the boiling water for 3 minutes, or until tender-crisp. Drain and cool slightly. Cut into thin slivers.

Heat 1 tablespoon of the oil in a large skillet over medium heat. Add the onion and cook for 4 minutes, or until soft. Add the garlic and cook for 2 minutes. Place in a large bowl and cool slightly.

Add the snap peas, potatoes, cheese, flour, salt, and pepper to the bowl. Stir until well-blended. Shape into 8 round cakes.

Heat 1½ tablespoons of the remaining oil in the same skillet over medium heat. Add 4 cakes and cook for 8 minutes, turning once, or until browned and heated through. Remove the cakes to a plate and keep warm. Repeat with the remaining cakes.

Evenly divide the mesclun and carrot curls among 4 plates and top with the cakes.

Makes 4 servings

Per serving: 385 calories, 12 g protein, 31 g carbohydrates, 24 g fat, 32 mg cholesterol, 2 g fiber, 801 mg sodium

CHEESE AND HERB STUFFED ARTICHOKES

4	medium artichokes		Salt
8	ounces soft goat cheese (such as chèvre)		Freshly ground black pepper
2	garlic cloves, minced	1	tablespoon olive oil
2	tablespoons chopped fresh chives		Juice of 1 large lemon
1	tablespoon chopped fresh oregano		

Place a steamer basket in a large pot with 2" of water. Bring to a boil over high heat.

Using scissors, trim off the sharp tips of the outer leaves of the artichokes. Place in the steamer basket and steam for 25 to 35 minutes, or until tender. Remove and turn upside down on a plate to cool slightly.

Preheat the oven to 375°F. Gently open the center of the artichokes. Using a teaspoon, remove and discard the inner chokes and thistles.

In a small bowl, combine the cheese, garlic, chives, and oregano. Season with salt and pepper. Evenly divide the cheese mixture among the cavities of the artichokes. Press the leaves back together and rub gently with the oil. Season with salt and pepper to taste and squeeze the lemon juice over the artichokes.

Place the artichokes in a shallow pan and bake for 15 minutes, or until heated through. Cut each artichoke in half and dip the leaves into the cheese mixture.

Makes 4 servings

Per serving: 255 calories, 15 g protein, 18 g carbohydrates, 16 g fat, 26 mg cholesterol, 8 g fiber, 331 mg sodium

This recipe was inspired by Nancy Gaffney, owner of Sea Star Goat Cheese Ranch in the Santa Cruz Mountains of California. Artichokes are one of those vegetables that are not easy to grow organically because the bugs love to hide in the leaves. That's probably why the organically grown ones are usually more expensive.

This simple recipe works with both wild mushrooms or domestic buttons. At Flea St. Café, we are lucky enough to know a few local mushroom foragers who bring us treasures through the back door of our kitchen. It may seem wasteful to use expensive mushrooms in soup, but it's a great way of stretching the expense and still maintaining deep, enticing flavors.

KITCHEN TIP

A combination of mushrooms works well. I like shiitakes mixed with regular button mushrooms. Or, when wild mushrooms are available, consider a combination of the somewhat mild chanterelles with a porcini or other full-flavored mushroom.

CREAM OF MUSHROOM SOUP

3 tablespoons butter	2 cups milk
1 onion, finely chopped	½ cup sour cream
24 ounces mushrooms (such as button, shiitake, cremini, and porcini), coarsley chopped	2–3 tablespoons chopped fresh parsley
⅓ cup unbleached all-purpose flour	1 teaspoon paprika
	Salt
3 cups vegetable or chicken broth	Freshly ground black pepper

Melt the butter in a large saucepan over medium heat. Add the onion and mushrooms and cook, stirring occasionally, for 7 minutes, or until very soft.

Sprinkle with the flour. Cook, stirring frequently, for 3 minutes. Gradually add the broth and simmer, stirring occasionally, for 5 minutes, or until the soup thickens.

Add the milk, sour cream, parsley, and paprika. Cook, stirring occasionally, for 3 minutes, or until heated through. Season with salt and pepper to taste.

Makes 6 servings

Per serving: 421 calories, 17 g protein, 60 g carbohydrates, 15 g fat, 35 mg cholesterol, 1 g fiber, 452 mg sodium

WHITE VEGETABLE LASAGNA

12	ounces lasagna noodles		16	ounces ricotta cheese
2	tablespoons olive oil		8	ounces mozzarella cheese, cut into small chunks
2	cups firmly packed very finely sliced red or green chard		½	cup (2 ounces) grated aged provolone cheese
2	shallots, minced		1	large egg, beaten
2	tablespoons unbleached all-purpose flour		2	tablespoons chopped fresh oregano
4	cups milk		3	tablespoons chopped fresh Italian parsley
¼	teaspoon freshly grated nutmeg		½	teaspoon salt
½	cup (2 ounces) grated Parmesan cheese		¼	teaspoon freshly ground black pepper

Preheat the oven to 375°F. Lightly coat a 13" × 9" baking dish with oil.

Cook the lasagna according to package directions. Drain and rinse under cold water. Drain completely.

Meanwhile, heat the oil in a medium saucepan over medium heat. Add the chard and shallots and cook for 4 minutes, or until soft. Using a slotted spoon, remove to a large bowl. Whisk the flour into the liquid and cook, stirring frequently, for 3 minutes. Gradually whisk in the milk and cook, stirring often, for 15 minutes, or until the sauce reaches a simmer and thickens. Stir in the chard, shallots, nutmeg, and Parmesan. Simmer for 1 minute.

In a medium bowl, combine the ricotta, mozzarella, provolone, egg, oregano, parsley, salt, and pepper.

Spread one-quarter of the chard sauce on the bottom of the prepared baking dish. Layer one-third of the lasagna on the sauce. Spread one-third of the ricotta mixture on top of the lasagna. Spread another one-quarter of the sauce over the cheese mixture. Repeat with the remaining lasagna, ricotta, and sauce.

Bake for 45 minutes, or until golden brown on top and heated through. Let stand for 10 minutes before serving.

Makes 12 servings

Per serving: 307 calories, 17 g protein, 20 g carbohydrates, 18 g fat, 71 mg cholesterol, 1 g fiber, 386 mg sodium

My oldest son, Joshua, loves this lasagna. When we feel like splurging, we mound lots of fresh crabmeat on top, creating a dish that he begs for when he wants me to cook him something special.

This may sound like an upscale restaurant dish, but it is actually very easy to prepare and would make an impressive meal for a dinner party. To have more time with your guests, make the potatoes and sauce ahead of time and then reheat before serving.

KITCHEN TIPS

You can buy coarsely ground pepper, but when freshly grated, the flavor is superior. I like to use a combination of red, green, and black peppercorns. Look for this mix, often sold as peppercorn mélange, in most supermarkets.

Smashed potatoes are much coarser than creamy mashed ones and always have the skin as well as the potato flesh. Not only delicious, but nutritious as well.

FILET MIGNON WITH SMASHED POTATOES AND LEEK SAUCE

4	filet mignon steaks (about 5 ounces each)	2	large leeks, whites only, sliced
½	teaspoon salt	½	cup hearty red wine (such as zinfandel or Cabernet)
4	tablespoons coarsely ground black pepper	1	tablespoon capers
1	pound new potatoes	1	tablespoon chopped fresh tarragon
¼–½	cup buttermilk		
3	tablespoons chopped fresh chives	2	tablespoons chopped fresh parsley
3	tablespoons butter		

Preheat the grill or broiler. Lightly oil the grill rack or broiler pan.

Rub the steaks with the salt, then press the pepper into both sides of the steaks. Refrigerate until ready to cook.

Bring a large pot of salted water to a boil. Add the potatoes and cook for 15 minutes, or until tender. Drain and place in a large bowl. Mash the potatoes with a potato masher or fork, adding the buttermilk until moist. Add the chives, cover, and keep warm.

Meanwhile, in a medium saucepan over medium heat, melt the butter and cook the leeks for 6 minutes, or until very soft. Add the wine, capers, and tarragon. Simmer for 3 minutes, or until well-blended and heated through. Keep warm.

Grill or broil the steaks for 15 minutes, turning once, until a thermometer inserted in the center registers 145°F for medium-rare.

To serve, evenly divide the potatoes and steaks among 4 plates. Top with the sauce. Sprinkle with the parsley.

Makes 4 servings

Per serving: 660 calories, 30 g protein, 34 g carbohydrates, 43 g fat, 126 mg cholesterol, 4 g fiber, 580 mg sodium

ZESTY ASPARAGUS AND SCALLOPS

3 tablespoons extra virgin olive oil

3 tablespoons fresh lime juice

2 tablespoons sugar

2 garlic cloves, minced

1 whole canned chipotle chile pepper, pureed or minced

3 tablespoons finely chopped fresh cilantro

1 pound asparagus, trimmed

1 pound sea scallops

¾ cup yellow cornmeal

1 teaspoon dried coriander

½ teaspoon salt

¼ teaspoon freshly ground black pepper

2 tablespoons butter

Lime wedges

In a small bowl, combine the oil, lime juice, sugar, garlic, chile pepper, and cilantro. Let sit for at least 30 minutes.

Meanwhile, place ½ cup water in a large skillet. Bring to a boil over high heat. Add the asparagus. Reduce the heat to medium-low, cover, and simmer for 4 minutes, or until tender-crisp. Remove to a platter and keep warm.

Remove and discard the tough muscle from the scallops.

In a small bowl, combine the cornmeal, coriander, salt, and black pepper. Dust the scallops with the cornmeal mixture.

In a heavy skillet over medium heat, melt the butter. Add the scallops and cook for 2 to 4 minutes, turning once, until lightly browned and opaque.

Evenly divide the asparagus among 4 plates. Top with the scallops. Drizzle with the chipotle dressing. Garnish with lime wedges.

Makes 4 servings

Per serving: 394 calories, 23 g protein, 31 g carbohydrates, 21 g fat, 52 mg cholesterol, 4 g fiber, 853 mg sodium

This is a perfect dish for springtime. If you live near a seacoast that catches scallops, try to find those that are naturally harvested or not bleached or treated with chemicals to lighten them. These are known as day boat scallops and are available in some fish markets and supermarkets. They may not look as uniform in size or color, but they are worth the extra cost for both health and environmental reasons.

In this recipe, any bold-tasting wild mushroom will work. I like chanterelles, porcini, or morels. If you can't find wild mushrooms in your market, shiitakes work great, and organic ones are plentiful.

KITCHEN TIP

Canned white beans will work for this recipe. Use one 14-ounce can, drained. Add as directed, but simmer for only 15 minutes.

SPRINGTIME CASSOULET

2	tablespoons olive oil
3	shallots, thinly sliced
8	ounces wild mushrooms, thinly sliced
2	garlic cloves, minced
1	cup small dry white beans, soaked overnight and drained (see tip)
2	sprigs fresh thyme
3	cups chicken broth
¾	pound sausage links (such as pork, chicken, or lamb), cut into ½" slices
3	small spring onions, whites and greens sliced into ½" pieces
	Salt
	Freshly ground black pepper
½	cup chopped fresh Italian parsley
½	cup (2 ounces) grated or shaved Parmesan or Asiago cheese

Heat the oil in a large skillet over medium heat. Add the shallots, mushrooms, and garlic and cook for 5 minutes, or until soft. Add the beans and brown lightly. Add the thyme and broth. Bring to a boil over high heat. Reduce the heat to low, cover, and simmer for 60 minutes, or until the beans are tender. Remove and discard the thyme sprig.

Meanwhile, heat another large skillet over medium-high heat. Add the sausage and onions and cook, stirring often, for 10 minutes, or until browned and the sausage is cooked through. Add to the bean mixture when the beans are tender. Season with salt and pepper to taste. Stir in the parsley. Top with the cheese.

Makes 6 servings

Per serving: 337 calories, 18 g protein, 24 g carbohydrates, 20 g fat, 35 mg cholesterol, 7 g fiber, 728 mg sodium

ORANGE-STEAMED CHICKEN AND ASPARAGUS

1	cup brown rice	1	tablespoon brown sugar
3	blood oranges	½	teaspoon salt
1	tablespoon extra virgin olive oil	4	bone-in chicken breast halves, skinned
2	garlic cloves, minced	16	asparagus spears, trimmed
3	tablespoons chopped fresh mint	12	green onions
		2	cups chicken broth
3	tablespoons chopped fresh chives	¼	teaspoon saffron threads (optional)

straightforward and easy, this light spring dish is a wonderfully delicious healthy meal that is very satisfying. It is perfect with blood oranges, but you can substitute any juicing orange if you cannot find blood oranges.

Cook the rice according to package directions.

Meanwhile, in a large shallow bowl, squeeze the oranges to yield ½ cup juice. Add the oil, garlic, mint, chives, brown sugar, and salt. Add the chicken, asparagus, and 8 of the onions. Toss to coat well. Cover and refrigerate for 30 minutes.

In a large saucepan over medium-high heat, bring the broth, saffron (if using), and the remaining 4 onions to a boil. Place a steamer basket or wire rack in the pan. Top with the chicken. Place the asparagus and onions over the chicken. Pour the marinade over the vegetables.

Return to a boil. Reduce the heat to medium-low, cover, and simmer for 20 minutes, or until a thermometer inserted in the thickest portion of a chicken breast registers 170°F and the juices run clear. Place the rice on a large platter. Arrange the chicken and vegetables over the rice and keep warm.

Remove the steamer basket and bring the cooking liquid to a boil over high heat. Boil for 10 minutes, or until the liquid has reduced by half. Remove and discard the onions.

Pour the liquid over the chicken and rice.

Makes 4 servings

Per serving: 292 calories, 32 g protein, 28 g carbohydrates, 6 g fat, 68 mg cholesterol, 5 g fiber, 669 mg sodium

LAMB CHOPS WITH STRAWBERRY-RHUBARB SAUCE

4 lamb rib or loin chops (about 2½ ounces each)

2 garlic cloves, minced

2 tablespoons finely chopped fresh rosemary

¼ teaspoon salt

¼ teaspoon freshly ground black pepper

2 teaspoons olive oil

½ small red onion, thinly sliced

¼ pound rhubarb, thinly sliced

2 tablespoons ruby port or balsamic vinegar

¾ cup strawberries, sliced

¼ cup sugar

¼ teaspoon freshly grated nutmeg

Preheat the broiler.

Place the chops on a broiler pan and rub with the garlic, rosemary, salt, and pepper. Set aside.

Heat the oil in a medium saucepan over medium heat. Add the onion and cook for 5 minutes, or until soft. Add the rhubarb and cook for 6 minutes, or until the rhubarb is soft. Add the port or vinegar and cook for 2 minutes.

Add the strawberries, sugar, and nutmeg. Reduce the heat to low and simmer for 5 minutes, or until well-blended.

Meanwhile, broil the chops for 5 minutes, turning once, until browned and a thermometer inserted in the center registers 145°F for medium-rare.

Serve the chops with the sauce.

Makes 4 servings

Per serving: 316 calories, 23 g protein, 21 g carbohydrates, 15 g fat, 74 mg cholesterol, 3 g fiber, 220 mg sodium

These lamb chops are wonderful with steamed rice tossed with slivered almonds and chopped chives.

KITCHEN TIP

Because of the short cooking time in this recipe, use tender greens, such as chard, spinach, or beet greens.

CHICKEN AND ORZO STEW

- 6 ounces orzo
- 1½ teaspoons whole mustard seeds
- 2 tablespoons extra virgin olive oil
- 1 pound boneless, skinless chicken breasts, cut into thin strips
- 1 red onion, thinly sliced
- 5 garlic cloves, minced
- 1 small apple, peeled and thinly sliced
- ½ cup dry white wine
- 2 cups chicken broth
- 3 tablespoons chopped fresh oregano
- 1 pound cooking greens, thinly sliced

Salt

Freshly ground black pepper

Grated Asiago or Parmesan cheese

Cook the orzo according to package directions. Drain and place in a large serving bowl.

Meanwhile, place the mustard seeds in a large skillet over medium heat. Cook, shaking the skillet often, for 5 minutes, or until lightly browned and toasted. Remove to the bowl with the orzo.

Heat the oil in the same skillet over medium-high heat. Add the chicken and cook, stirring frequently, for 5 minutes, or until browned and cooked through. Remove with a slotted spoon to the bowl with the orzo.

Add the onion to the skillet and cook for 4 minutes, or until soft. Add the garlic and cook for 2 minutes. Add the apple, wine, broth, oregano, and greens. Cover and simmer for 5 minutes, stirring occasionally, or until the greens are wilted. Season with salt and pepper to taste and add to the bowl with the orzo and chicken. Toss to blend well.

Garnish with the cheese.

Makes 6 servings

Per serving: 336 calories, 29 g protein, 32 g carbohydrates, 9 g fat, 85 mg cholesterol, 5 g fiber, 615 mg sodium

PRUNE AND FENNEL SALAD

3	tablespoons extra virgin olive oil	¼	teaspoon freshly ground black pepper
	Juice of 1 lemon	1	large fennel bulb, thinly sliced
2	tablespoons chopped fresh dill	1	small red onion, thinly sliced
2	tablespoons honey	1	cup pitted prunes, sliced
¼	teaspoon salt		

In a medium bowl, whisk together the oil, lemon juice, dill, honey, salt, and pepper. Add the fennel, onion, and prunes. Toss to coat well. Marinate at room temperature for at least 1 hour. Serve immediately or refrigerate to serve later.

Makes 6 servings

Per serving: 191 calories, 2 g protein, 35 g carbohydrates, 7 g fat, 0 mg cholesterol, 5 g fiber, 43 mg sodium

Simple yet flavorful, this salad improves overnight, so try to make it a day ahead. If prunes aren't your cup of tea, substitute raisins or dried apricots.

KITCHEN TIP

Celery may be used in place of the fennel, or try a combination of both.

For this salad, it is best to use those overripe strawberries, the ones you consider throwing away because they are so soft and juicy. To make the puree, use a food processor or blender. Or, for a chunky strawberry vinaigrette, mash them with a fork.

WATERCRESS WITH STRAWBERRY VINAIGRETTE AND CHEDDAR CROUTONS

Croutons

6	ounces smoked Cheddar cheese	¾	teaspoon ground red pepper (optional)
1	egg	½	teaspoon salt
½	cup unbleached all-purpose flour		

Salad

16	strawberries	½	teaspoon salt
3	tablespoons extra virgin olive oil	¼	teaspoon freshly ground black pepper
3	tablespoons balsamic vinegar	8	cups watercress
1	garlic clove, minced	1	avocado, halved, pitted, peeled, and sliced
2	teaspoons chopped fresh thyme	1	green onion, finely chopped

To make the croutons: Preheat the oven to 350°F. Lightly oil a baking sheet.

Cut the cheese into ½" squares.

In a small bowl, beat the egg with 2 tablespoons cold water. In another small bowl, combine the flour, pepper (if using), and salt. Working in batches, use your hands or tongs to toss the cheese in the flour. Then toss in the beaten egg and coat thoroughly. Toss again in the flour. Place on the prepared baking sheet. Bake for 15 minutes, or until lightly browned.

To make the salad: Meanwhile, place 12 of the strawberries in a food processor or blender and process until pureed. (You should have ½ cup.) Slice the remaining 4 strawberries and set aside.

In a large bowl, whisk together the strawberry puree, oil, vinegar, garlic, thyme, salt, and pepper.

Add the watercress to the bowl with the vinaigrette; toss to coat well.

Evenly divide the watercress among 6 plates. Arrange the avocado on the plates and top with the green onion, sliced strawberries, and croutons.

Makes 6 servings
Per serving: 291 calories, 11 g protein, 15 g carbohydrates, 21 g fat, 65 mg cholesterol, 5 g fiber, 588 mg sodium

Nora Pouillon

Restaurant Nora and **Asia Nora**, Washington, D.C.

Courtesy of Mahdavian/Restaurant Nora

Organic food became important to me when, as a young bride, I came to this country in the 1960s and realized how far agricultural practices differed from the ones I grew up with in Austria. I truly believe that food affects both our health and that of our planet, and the healing aspect of food in America had been completely lost. We are what we eat. And so began my search for and commitment to organic food, which I have carried from my home kitchen to my restaurants.

ASPARAGUS WITH FROTHY HOLLANDAISE

2   pounds asparagus, trimmed

2   large organic eggs, separated

2   teaspoons lemon juice

2   teaspoons white wine vinegar

4   ounces butter

Pinch of cayenne pepper

Salt and freshly ground black pepper to taste

Grill or steam the asparagus until tender.

Blend the egg yolks and some salt in a food processor until well-combined.

In a small saucepan, heat the lemon juice and vinegar until simmering and, with the machine still running, pour the hot liquid on the egg yolk and salt mixture. Switch off the machine.

Using the same pan, now melt the butter gently and, when it is foaming, with the processor switched on again, add the melted butter in a steady stream until it is incorporated and the mixture has thickened.

In a clean, dry bowl, whisk the egg whites until they form soft peaks, then gently fold in the egg mixture, 1 tablespoon at a time, until well-combined. Check for seasoning and serve immediately or refrigerate overnight.

Add 1 to 2 tablespoons of French tarragon, and you nearly have béarnaise sauce—another traditional sauce to serve with meat, poultry, or fish.

Makes 8 servings

BALSAMIC ASPARAGUS WITH CHEESE TOASTS

1½ pounds asparagus, trimmed

¼ cup balsamic vinegar

1 tablespoon tamari or soy sauce

3 tablespoons brown sugar

2 garlic cloves, minced

1 green onion, sliced

8 ounces cream cheese, softened

2 tablespoons chopped fresh chives

2 tablespoons chopped fresh tarragon

1 small whole grain Italian bread, diagonally cut into 12 slices (about 1") and toasted

Salt

Freshly ground black pepper

6 radishes, thinly sliced

For me, this dish is the essence of springtime. It can be served cold as a first course or salad. Or, keep the asparagus and sauce warm and use as a side dish with poached or grilled salmon.

Place ½ cup water in a large skillet. Bring to a boil over high heat. Add the asparagus. Reduce the heat to medium-low, cover, and simmer for 4 minutes, or until tender-crisp. Rinse under cold water. Drain.

Meanwhile, in a small saucepan, combine the vinegar, tamari or soy sauce, brown sugar, garlic, onion, and 2 tablespoons water. Bring to a boil over high heat. Reduce the heat to medium and cook for 10 minutes, or until reduced by half.

In a small bowl, combine the cream cheese, chives, and tarragon. Spread the bread slices with the cream cheese mixture. Season with salt and pepper to taste. Arrange the radishes on top.

Arrange the asparagus on a large platter or 6 individual salad plates. Drizzle with the vinegar mixture. Place the cheese toasts around the asparagus.

Makes 6 servings

Per serving: 222 calories, 8 g protein, 18 g carbohydrates, 14 g fat, 42 mg cholesterol, 4 g fiber, 225 mg sodium

SPRING VEGETABLE SAUTÉ

¾	pound new potatoes, cut in half	½	teaspoon freshly grated nutmeg
½	pound sugar snap peas, trimmed	2–3	tablespoons chopped fresh mint
2	tablespoons butter		Salt
3–4	small spring onions, thinly sliced		Freshly ground black pepper
2	garlic cloves, minced		

Place a large pot of salted water over high heat and bring to a boil. Add the potatoes and cook for 20 minutes, or until tender. Add the snap peas during the last 2 minutes of cooking time. Drain.

Heat the butter in a large skillet over medium heat. Add the onions and garlic and cook for 5 minutes, or until tender. Add the potatoes, snap peas, nutmeg, and mint. Toss to coat well. Season with salt and pepper to taste.

Makes 6 servings

Per serving: 103 calories, 3 g protein, 15 g carbohydrates, 4 g fat, 11 mg cholesterol, 2 g fiber, 54 mg sodium

For me, spring has really begun when I go to the market and find sugar snap peas. In a basket nearby, you'll most likely find freshly dug new potatoes and fragrant spring onions. Bringing them together in a dish as simple as this seems only natural.

At times, I like vegetables cooked until they are very soft, forming a soup of sorts with a savory yet most often simple broth. The stock adds dimension and flavor without relying on olive oil or butter. This comforting health food is found in my refrigerator often.

STEAMED BOK CHOY AND WATER CHESTNUTS

1½	pounds bok choy		½	cup chopped fresh cilantro
2	cups vegetable or chicken broth		2	tablespoons tamari or soy sauce
2	garlic cloves, minced			Salt
1	small onion, thinly sliced			Freshly ground black pepper
½	orange, cut into wedges			
1	can (4 ounces) sliced water chestnuts, drained			

If the bok choy heads are small, cut into halves or quarters. If it is a large head, chop into bite-size pieces.

In a medium saucepan over high heat, bring the broth, garlic, onion, and orange wedges to a boil. Reduce the heat to low, cover, and simmer for 5 minutes. Add the bok choy and simmer for 5 minutes, or until tender. Add the water chestnuts, cilantro, and tamari or soy sauce. Simmer for 1 minute. Remove and discard the orange wedges. Season with salt and pepper to taste. Serve in bowls.

Makes 6 servings

Per serving: 38 calories, 4 g protein, 8 g carbohydrates, 0 g fat, 0 mg cholesterol, 3 g fiber, 635 mg sodium

RYE, ONION, AND SWISS CHEESE MUFFINS

1	cup milk	1	cup rye flour
1	large egg	2	tablespoons sugar
1	small red onion, minced	1	tablespoon baking powder
2	tablespoons vegetable oil	½	teaspoon salt
1	cup whole grain pastry flour	1	cup (4 ounces) shredded Swiss cheese

Preheat the oven to 400°F. Oil a 12-cup muffin pan or 1 baking sheet.

In a medium bowl, combine the milk, egg, onion, and oil.

In another medium bowl, combine the pastry flour, rye flour, sugar, baking powder, and salt. Form a well in the center and add the milk mixture and cheese. Stir just until blended.

Evenly divide among the prepared muffin cups or drop 12 spoonfuls onto the prepared baking sheet.

Bake for 20 minutes, or until a wooden pick inserted in the center of a muffin comes out clean.

Makes 12

Per serving: 196 calories, 9 g protein, 19 g carbohydrates, 9 g fat, 41 mg cholesterol, 1 g fiber, 240 mg sodium

I actually like to bake these muffins free form, dropped like biscuits onto a well-oiled baking sheet. Split in half and stuffed with thin slices of meat, lettuce, red onion, and a generous smear of honey mustard, they're heavenly. Of course, they are meant to be baked in well-oiled or lined muffin tins and served with butter or cream cheese, which is also quite delicious.

KITCHEN TIP

For a heartier breakfast muffin, add ½ cup cooked and crumbled meat or veggie sausage to the batter with the cheese.

KITCHEN TIP

This pudding can be changed to fit your tastes for the day. For a lighter version, use low-fat ricotta cheese. For a richer pudding, substitute sour cream for the yogurt.

CHERRY-CHEESE PUDDING

½	cup dried cherries or golden raisins	½	cup sugar
3	large eggs	1	teaspoon vanilla extract
24	ounces ricotta cheese	½	teaspoon freshly grated nutmeg
1	cup low-fat plain yogurt		

Preheat the oven to 350°F. Fill a large baking dish with 2 cups water. Butter eight 6-ounce ramekins or one 1-quart baking dish. Scatter the cherries or raisins on the bottom.

Separate the eggs, placing the whites in a medium bowl and the yolks in a large bowl.

Beat the egg whites with an electric mixer on high speed until soft peaks form. Set aside.

Add the ricotta, yogurt, sugar, and vanilla extract to the bowl with the egg yolks. Using the same beaters, beat the mixture until smooth. Fold the egg whites into the ricotta mixture.

Pour into the prepared ramekins or baking dish. Sprinkle the nutmeg on the top. Place in the baking dish with the water. Bake for 30 minutes, or until a knife inserted in the center comes out clean. Cool completely on a rack.

Serve at room temperature or refrigerate to serve cold later.

Makes 8 servings

Per serving: 276 calories, 14 g protein, 25 g carbohydrates, 14 g fat, 125 mg cholesterol, 1 g fiber, 118 mg sodium

RASPBERRY MILLET PANCAKES

We all like warm desserts, right out of the oven. An easy and quick way to make a sweet cake to order is in the form of a pancake. If you have a terrible sweet tooth, add more maple syrup or even sugar to the batter. Serve with sour cream or vanilla frozen yogurt or ice cream.

⅓	cup millet	1½	cups unbleached all-purpose flour
1	cup water	1½	teaspoons baking soda
2	eggs	1	teaspoon ground cinnamon
1½	cups buttermilk	½	teaspoon salt
¼	cup pure maple syrup	1	pint raspberries
2	tablespoons vegetable oil	1	pint vanilla frozen yogurt
1	teaspoon vanilla extract		

Place the millet in a medium saucepan over medium heat. Cook, shaking the skillet often, for 3 minutes, or until lightly browned and toasted. Add the water and bring to a boil over high heat. Reduce the heat to low, cover, and simmer for 15 minutes, or until the liquid is absorbed. Remove from the heat, but do not remove the cover, and let stand for 15 minutes. Cool to room temperature.

Meanwhile, in a medium bowl, combine the eggs, buttermilk, maple syrup, oil, and vanilla extract.

In a large bowl, combine the flour, baking soda, cinnamon, and salt. Form a well in the center of the flour mixture and stir in the buttermilk mixture just until blended. Add the millet, stirring to blend.

Lightly oil a griddle or large skillet and heat over medium-high heat. Drop the batter by scant ¼ cups onto the griddle or skillet. Cook for 3 minutes, or until the uncooked side begins to bubble. Flip and cook for 2 minutes longer, or until browned.

To serve, place 3 pancakes on each plate. Top with the raspberries and frozen yogurt.

Makes 6 servings

Per serving: 377 calories, 11 g protein, 61 g carbohydrates, 10 g fat, 80 mg cholesterol, 4 g fiber, 616 mg sodium

BANANA-WALNUT SHORTBREAD

2½ cups whole grain pastry flour	¾ cup packed brown sugar
½ teaspoon baking powder	1 large very ripe banana, mashed
⅛ teaspoon salt	1 teaspoon vanilla extract
1½ cups unsalted butter, softened	½ cup chopped walnuts

Preheat the oven to 400°F.

In a medium bowl, combine the flour, baking powder, and salt.

In a large bowl with an electric mixer, beat the butter and brown sugar until creamy. Add the banana and vanilla extract, beating just until incorporated. Add the flour mixture and beat just until well-blended. Stir in the nuts.

Divide the dough into quarters. Press one-quarter of the dough into an 8" circle on a large baking sheet. Using the dull side of a knife, press into the dough, forming 12 pie-shaped wedges. Crimp the ends, if desired. Repeat with a second quarter of the dough on the same baking sheet. Shape the remaining quarters of dough on another large baking sheet.

Bake for 20 minutes, or until lightly browned and the shortbread rises. Place on racks to cool.

Makes 48

Per serving: 102 calories, 1 g protein, 10 g carbohydrates, 7 g fat, 16 mg cholesterol, 0 g fiber, 14 mg sodium

I like simple desserts, especially those that are versatile. These "cookies" stand on their own and can easily be made more glorious when served next to bowls of fresh strawberries or chocolate ice cream.

STRAWBERRY-CHOCOLATE COBBLER

½	cup unsalted butter	2	teaspoons baking powder
⅓	cup unsweetened cocoa powder	1	teaspoon ground cinnamon
1	cup sugar	1	cup milk
2	cups whole grain pastry flour	1	pint strawberries, hulled and sliced

Preheat the oven to 350°F.

Place the butter, cocoa, and ¼ cup of the sugar in a 3-quart glass baking dish. Place in the oven for 3 to 5 minutes to melt the butter. Remove from the oven and stir until well-blended.

Meanwhile, in a medium bowl, combine the flour, baking powder, cinnamon, and the remaining ¾ cup sugar. Add the milk and stir until the mixture is smooth. Spoon onto the melted butter mixture, but do not stir.

Sprinkle with the strawberries. Bake for 45 to 55 minutes, or until a wooden pick inserted in the center comes out clean.

Let stand for 15 minutes before serving.

Makes 6 servings

Per serving: 360 calories, 6 g protein, 54 g carbohydrates, 14 g fat, 37 mg cholesterol, 2 g fiber, 119 mg sodium

This standard cobbler recipe makes good use of the first fresh fruit of spring: strawberries. I like to serve it warm with vanilla ice cream and hot fudge sauce.

KITCHEN TIP

Consider this cobbler in the winter, using whole frozen organic berries.

LATE SPRING

By mid-April, my mind, my soul, and my tastebuds are ready for light, bright spring flavors to step up to the plate. Late spring is a time of transition. The pavement is dry, but a hint of coolness remains. The air delivers a fresh, warm, floral scent from the many blooms of roses and edible, colorful flowers. Baby root vegetables like turnips and carrots announce their arrival.

The weather is predictably unpredictable. Days waiver from rainy and chilly to dry and warm. I find myself catering to these climate changes in my kitchen. On cool, damp days, I am filled with the desire to prepare warm, meaty dishes. When the sun dominates the day, I shift to lighter, fresher fare whose flavors are on the brink of ripeness. I rejoice in the spring harvest that provides me with the gifts of salad greens, berries, artichokes, mushrooms, and fresh herbs.

The weather also affects me physically. I find it difficult to exercise during cold spring days, rebelliously resisting gyms. A few pounds are  gained as I satisfy my craving for fattier foods. On sunny spring days, the outdoors beckons me, and I find myself enthusiastically walking the challenging hills near my home to expend some calories and to meditate.

There's no argument that exercise, diet, and joyfulness are keys to keeping one healthy. Springtime simply makes it easier to keep one in balance physically, mentally, and spiritually.

Recipes

GARLIC ARTICHOKES OVER GRUYÈRE TOASTS

4	cups vegetable or chicken broth	2	tablespoons chopped fresh oregano
2	tablespoons extra virgin olive oil	1	tablespoon lemon zest
			Salt
8	baby artichokes, trimmed and halved		Freshly ground black pepper
4	green garlic bulbs or green onions, chopped	4	ounces Gruyère or Swiss cheese, sliced
½	fennel bulb, thinly sliced	4	slices Italian white bread
6	garlic cloves, minced	¼	cup chopped fresh parsley

In a medium saucepan over high heat, bring the broth to a boil. Reduce the heat to low, cover, and simmer.

Heat the oil in a large skillet over medium heat. Add the artichokes, green garlic or green onions, and fennel and cook for 5 minutes, or until the artichokes have browned slightly. Add the minced garlic, oregano, and lemon zest. Pour in 1 cup of the simmering broth. Cook, turning the artichokes often, over medium heat for 10 minutes, or until the liquid reduces. Keep adding broth until the artichokes are tender, about 10 minutes. Season with salt and pepper to taste. Set aside to cool.

Preheat the broiler.

Place the cheese on the bread. Place on a broiler pan and broil for 3 minutes, or until the cheese is melted and slightly browned. Cut the bread slices diagonally in half and place 2 halves in each of 4 shallow bowls.

Evenly divide the artichokes among the bowls. Sprinkle with the parsley.

Makes 4 servings

Per serving: 343 calories, 17 g protein, 34 g carbohydrates, 17 g fat, 31 mg cholesterol, 9 g fiber, 828 g sodium

KITCHEN TIP

For most people, asparagus is the first sign that spring has arrived. For me, when I first see green garlic, I know that winter is near its end. The beauty of green garlic, which is gentle in flavor, is that I use it not only raw but also tossed in as a last addition to many dishes, such as pastas, steamed vegetables, grains or, most delightful of all, scrambled eggs.

Typically, green garlic is young garlic that has not formed cloves. Because it is picked at different times of growth, it must be handled according to its size. If the bulb is immature and the size of a green onion, trim off the outer leaves and chop the whole thing. The more mature the bulb gets, meaning larger, then it must be thinly sliced according to size. Not always available in supermarkets, green garlic is plentiful at farmers' markets and looks similar to a green onion.

TUNA-STUFFED MUSHROOMS

Serve these mushrooms as an appetizer or as a main course for lunch or a picnic.

¼ cup vegetable broth

1 garlic clove, thinly sliced

2 tablespoons chopped fresh dill

16 large mushroom caps

1 tuna steak (6 ounces)

1 teaspoon lemon zest

1½ tablespoons lemon juice

2 tablespoons grated red onion

1 tablespoon capers

6 kalamata olives, pitted and chopped coarsely

2–3 tablespoons olive oil

Salt

Freshly ground black pepper

2 tablespoon chopped fresh chives

In a large skillet over high heat, bring the broth, garlic, and dill to a boil. Add the mushroom caps, reduce the heat to low, cover, and simmer for 3 minutes. Remove the mushroom caps and set aside, reserving the cooking liquid.

Place the tuna in the cooking liquid. Cover and simmer for 5 minutes, or until the fish is just opaque. Place the tuna in a medium bowl and cool slightly.

Mash the tuna. Add the lemon zest, lemon juice, onion, capers, and olives. Add enough oil to moisten. Season with salt and pepper to taste. Evenly divide the tuna salad among the mushroom caps. Sprinkle with the chives.

Makes 4 servings

Per serving: 186 calories, 12 g protein, 5 g carbohydrates, 14 g fat, 16 mg cholesterol, 1 g fiber, 196 mg sodium

KITCHEN TIP

For an elegant touch, place the wasabi cream in a small resealable plastic bag. Snip one corner of the bag and pipe the cream onto the soup. Use a wooden pick to create a decorative design.

CURRY CARROT SOUP WITH WASABI CREAM

3	tablespoons butter		1	tablespoon curry powder
2	large onions, thinly sliced		1–3	tablespoons honey
2	pounds carrots, thinly sliced			Salt
½	cup mirin cooking wine or apple juice			Freshly ground black pepper
6	cups vegetable or chicken broth		1	tablespoon wasabi powder
			1	cup (8 ounces) sour cream or yogurt
¼	cup grated fresh ginger		4	green onions, chopped

Melt the butter in a large soup pot over medium-high heat. Add the onions and cook for 5 minutes, or until soft. Add the carrots and wine or apple juice and cook for 3 minutes. Add the broth, ginger, and curry powder and bring to a boil.

Reduce the heat to low, cover, and simmer for 40 minutes, or until the carrots are very tender.

Remove from the heat. Working in batches, pour the soup into a food processor or blender. Process until smooth. Place in a soup tureen or large bowl. Stir in the honey and salt and pepper to taste.

While the soup is cooking, in a small bowl, blend the wasabi powder with the sour cream or yogurt. Stir in the green onions.

Ladle the soup into bowls and top with a generous spoonful of the wasabi cream. Swirl the cream into the soup.

Makes 8 servings
Per serving: 215 calories, 7 g protein, 30 g carbohydrates, 10 g fat, 23 mg cholesterol, 4 g fiber, 623 g sodium

I like to make this salad at different times of the year. It's delicious with oranges, but during the summer months, substitute apricots, peaches, or pitted cherries.

FRUITED CHICKEN SALAD

2   tablespoons olive oil

2   tablespoons sherry wine vinegar

2   tablespoons brown sugar

1   tablespoon Dijon mustard

1   small red onion, halved and thinly sliced

3   tablespoons chopped fresh mint

½   teaspoon salt

½   teaspoon freshly ground black pepper

2   oranges

½   cup pitted kalamata olives

1   pound cooked chicken breast, cut into thin strips

1   large head butter lettuce

In a medium bowl, whisk together the oil, vinegar, brown sugar, and mustard. Add the onion, mint, salt, and pepper and let stand at room temperature for 10 minutes.

Section the oranges over the bowl and add along with the olives and chicken. Toss to coat well.

Arrange the lettuce leaves on 4 plates. Spoon the salad onto the leaves.

Makes 4 servings

Per serving: 364 calories, 35 g protein, 20 g carbohydrates, 16 g fat, 87 mg cholesterol, 4 g fiber, 618 mg sodium

LAMB BURGERS WITH CARAMELIZED SHALLOTS

1	tablespoon olive oil	1	teaspoon finely chopped fresh rosemary
½	pound shallots, sliced	½	teaspoon salt
1	pound ground lamb	½	teaspoon freshly ground black pepper
½	red onion, grated	4	whole wheat buns
1	garlic clove, minced		

Heat the oil in a large skillet over medium-high heat. Add the shallots and cook, stirring occasionally, for 7 minutes, or until soft and golden brown. Remove to a bowl.

Meanwhile, in a medium bowl, combine the lamb, onion, garlic, rosemary, salt, and pepper. Form into 4 burgers.

In the same skillet over medium heat, cook the burgers for 10 minutes, turning once, or until a thermometer inserted in the center registers 145°F for medium-rare.

Place the burgers on the buns and top with the shallots.

Makes 4 servings

Per serving: 504 calories, 24 g protein, 29 g carbohydrates, 33 g fat, 91 mg cholesterol, 3 g fiber, 515 mg sodium

When I am hungry for meat, there is nothing that compares with a great burger. Of course, you can use ground beef, turkey, chicken, pork, or even a good meat substitute instead of the lamb. It is the oniony quality of both the caramelized shallots and the bits of onion in the meat that makes the difference for me.

BEEF STEW
WITH BABY SPRING
VEGETABLES

1½	pounds beef stew meat	6	garlic cloves, minced
8	whole small shallots	2	celery ribs, finely chopped
2	tablespoons garam masala	4	sprigs fresh thyme
1½	teaspoons salt	4	sprigs fresh Italian parsley
1	teaspoon freshly ground black pepper	1	bay leaf
		1	teaspoon ground cloves
8	cups assorted baby vegetables (carrots, beets, turnips, radishes, potatoes, fennel), about 40 pieces	2	teaspoons ground coriander
		6	cups beef or chicken broth

Even in springtime, there are cool nights when a comforting stew can't be beat. When possible, keep the vegetables whole, unless they are very large, then cut them into large bite-size pieces.

Preheat the oven to 500°F.

Place the meat and shallots in a deep large roasting pan. Sprinkle with the garam masala, ½ teaspoon of the salt, and ½ teaspoon of the pepper. Roast for 30 minutes, or until browned.

Reduce the heat to 350°F.

Add the baby vegetables, garlic, celery, thyme, parsley, bay leaf, cloves, coriander, the remaining 1 teaspoon salt, the remaining ½ teaspoon pepper, and broth. Stir to mix well.

Cover and roast, basting occasionally with the liquid, for 2½ to 3 hours, or until the meat is tender. Remove and discard the bay leaf and sprigs before serving.

Makes 8 servings
Per serving: 364 calories, 25 g protein, 15 g carbohydrates, 23 g fat, 79 mg cholesterol, 2 g fiber, 977 mg sodium

Cooked in your grandma's stew pot or a brand new Dutch oven, this dish comes together in no time, and it's a wonderful way to combine the best of the spring harvest. Homemade dumplings complete the meal wonderfully.

KITCHEN TIP

If you are not a dumpling fan, eliminate that step and serve the stew over rice or a similar cooked grain and garnish with lots of radishes.

CHICKEN STEW WITH RADISH DUMPLINGS

Stew

1	tablespoon olive oil	2	carrots, sliced
1	fennel bulb, sliced	2	tablespoons chopped fresh oregano
1	onion, sliced	½	cup Madeira wine
4	boneless, skinless chicken breasts, sliced into bite-size pieces	6	cups chicken broth
½	pound potatoes, peeled and cubed		

Dumplings

1	cup unbleached all-purpose flour	1	egg, beaten
½	teaspoon salt	½	cup minced radishes
3	tablespoons vegetable oil	2½	tablespoons cornstarch
3	tablespoons milk	½	cup water

To make the stew: Heat the oil in a Dutch oven over medium heat. Add the fennel, onion, and chicken and cook for 8 minutes, or until lightly browned.

Add the potatoes, carrots, oregano, wine, and broth to the pot. Bring to a boil over high heat. Reduce the heat to low and simmer for 30 minutes, or until tender.

To make the dumplings: Meanwhile, in a medium bowl, combine the flour and salt. In a small bowl, combine the oil, milk, egg, and radishes. Gradually add to the flour mixture to form a soft dough.

In a small bowl, dissolve the cornstarch in the water. Add to the simmering stew and cook for 2 minutes, or until thickened.

Using 2 teaspoons, drop the dumpling batter into the simmering stew. Cover and cook for 10 minutes, or until the dumplings are cooked through.

Makes 6 servings

Per serving: 417 calories, 33 g protein, 35 g carbohydrates, 14 g fat, 111 mg cholesterol, 3 g fiber, 876 mg sodium

SALMON EN PAPILLOTE

1	cup basmati or white rice	1½	tablespoon capers
1½	cups chicken broth or water	4	salmon fillets (about 1 pound total)
¼	cup chopped fresh mint		Salt
1	tablespoon olive oil		Freshly ground black pepper
½	teaspoon salt		Juice of 1 orange
4	ounces soft goat cheese (such as chèvre)	2	tablespoons finely chopped fresh chives
½	cup raisins		
⅛	teaspoon freshly grated nutmeg		

Steaming fish in parchment is a wonderful way to seal in juices and create a spectacular presentation. In addition, the packages can be put together ahead of time and popped in the oven just before dinner.

In a medium saucepan over high heat, bring the rice, broth or water, mint, oil, and salt to a boil. Reduce the heat to low, cover, and simmer for 20 minutes. Do not remove the lid. Remove from the heat and let stand, covered, for at least 10 minutes. Just before serving, fluff with a fork.

Meanwhile, preheat the oven to 450°F.

In a small bowl, combine the cheese, raisins, nutmeg, and capers.

Cut four 12" circles of parchment paper or foil. Rinse the salmon under cold water, pat dry, and place each on one half of the parchment or foil, about 1½" from the edge. Sprinkle each fillet with salt and pepper. Place one-quarter of the cheese mixture on top. Sprinkle with the orange juice and chives. Fold over the parchment and, starting at the edge of the half-circle using small folds, completely seal the fish and cheese mixture inside the parchment. Place on a baking sheet and bake for 15 minutes. Remove from the oven and place a packet on each of 4 plates. Tear through the parchment with a sharp-tipped knife. Serve with the rice.

Makes 4 servings
Per serving: 579 calories, 35 g protein, 52 g carbohydrates, 26 g fat, 88 mg cholesterol, 4 g fiber, 762 mg sodium

KITCHEN TIP

I also like to serve this fish chilled on top of a bed of salad greens. Or, pack it in a picnic basket along with a baguette for sandwiches in the park or on the beach.

RED SNAPPER WITH PARSLEY-ALMOND PESTO

1	cup firmly packed curly parsley, stems removed			Juice of 1 large lemon
1	garlic clove		¼	cup extra virgin olive oil (or enough to create a smooth, loose paste)
2	tablespoons slivered almonds		4	red snapper fillets (about 1½ pounds total)
¼	cup (1 ounce) grated Parmesan or Asiago cheese		1	teaspoon paprika

Preheat the broiler.

Place the parsley, garlic, almonds, and cheese in a food processor or blender. Pulse until pureed. Add the lemon juice. Gradually add the oil and puree until the sauce is smooth.

Brush both sides of the fillets with the pesto. Sprinkle with the paprika.

Lightly oil the broiler pan. Place the fillets on the pan and broil for 5 to 10 minutes, or until opaque.

Makes 4 servings

Per serving: 365 calories, 40 g protein, 5 g carbohydrates, 21 g fat, 68 mg cholesterol, 271 g fiber, 271 mg sodium

Michael Romano

Union Square Café, New York City

Courtesy of Union Square Café

Cooking with organic foods is conscious cooking. To the degree that we continue to cook with products, both of the land and from the Earth, that are not raised organically or at least in a sustainable manner, we are choosing to ignore the harmful long-term effect that this will have on our personal health and the health of our ecosystems. Raising consciousness and changing old, familiar habits is never easy. But in this case, do we really have a choice?

RISOTTO D'ORO

3	cups carrot juice
3	cups celery juice
¼	cup olive oil
1¾	cups Arborio rice
½	teaspoon minced garlic
½	cup white wine
½	cup peeled, split lengthwise, and sliced carrots
½	cup 1" pieces green beans
½	cup split lengthwise and sliced zucchini

½	cup ½" pieces asparagus, tough ends discarded
½	cup sliced red bell pepper
½	cup fresh shelled peas
⅓	cup sliced scallions
4	tablespoons butter
¾	cup finely grated Parmigiano Reggiano
1	teaspoon kosher salt
⅛	teaspoon freshly ground black pepper
1	tablespoon chopped parsley

In a saucepan, combine the carrot and celery juices and bring to a simmer.

In a 3-quart saucepan, heat the olive oil over medium heat. Add the rice and garlic and stir together until the rice is coated with the oil. Add the white wine and bring to a boil, stirring constantly, until the wine is absorbed by the rice. Add the carrots and the green beans to the rice.

Ladle ½ cup of the hot juice mixture into the saucepan and stir until it is absorbed. Continue with the rest of the juice, adding ½ cup at a time and letting each addition be absorbed completely into the rice before adding more liquid. The constant stirring allows the rice to release its starch into the cooking liquid, resulting in the characteristic risotto creaminess. When three-quarters of the juice has been used, about 15 to 20 minutes, stir in the remaining vegetables. Continue ladling and stirring in the remaining juice, about 10 additional minutes. The grains of rice should be al dente.

Swirl in the butter and three-quarters of the Parmigiano and season with the salt and pepper. Serve the risotto sprinkled with parsley and the remaining Parmigiano.

Makes 8 servings

RICOTTA–GREEN ONION GNOCCHI

15 ounces ricotta cheese

1 egg, beaten

½ teaspoon salt

½ teaspoon freshly ground black pepper

6 green onions, minced

½ cup (2 ounces) grated Asiago or Parmesan cheese

1½–2 cups unbleached all-purpose flour

3 cups pasta sauce

Place the ricotta in a sieve over a bowl for 15 to 30 minutes to drain. Discard the liquid.

Bring a large pot of salted water to a boil.

In a medium bowl, combine the drained ricotta, egg, salt, pepper, green onion, and cheese. Gradually add the flour, ¼ cup at a time, using your hands and blending just until the dough holds together. Remove 1 teaspoon of the dough and roll into a ball on a floured surface. Drop into the boiling water. If the piece falls apart, add more flour to the dough, 2 tablespoons at a time, until the dough forms a ball. Repeat the cooking test until the gnocchi holds together and floats to the surface.

Divide the dough into 4 equal parts. On a generously floured board, using your hands, roll each section into a rope about 1" in diameter. Cut the ropes into 1" pieces and slightly indent with a fork. Thoroughly cover with flour and store in the refrigerator or freezer until ready to use.

Drop the gnocchi into the boiling water. Stir gently to prevent sticking. When the gnocchi float to the top, they are cooked.

Meanwhile, heat the sauce in a medium saucepan over medium heat. Drain the gnocchi and place in a serving bowl. Top with the sauce.

Makes 4 servings

Per serving: 557 calories, 27 g protein, 58 g carbohydrates, 23 g fat, 117 mg cholesterol, 2 g fiber, 1,100 mg sodium

Gnocchi have become an all-time favorite around my house. I typically make far more than can be eaten at one meal. They freeze well and can be taken from the freezer and dropped directly into boiling water to cook. Try these gnocchi with a simple red sauce or drizzled with olive oil, garlic, parsley, and lots of grated Italian cheese.

POTATO AND SPINACH STUFFED PASTA

12	cannelloni, manicotti, or large shells	2	bunches fresh spinach, chopped; or 2 boxes (10 ounces each) frozen chopped spinach, thawed and squeezed dry
¾	pound potatoes, peeled and cubed	8	ounces smoked mozzarella cheese
3	tablespoons extra virgin olive oil		Salt
1	onion, thinly sliced		Freshly ground black pepper
3	garlic cloves, minced	1	jar (26 ounces) pasta sauce
2	tablespoons chopped fresh oregano		Chopped fresh Italian parsley
¼	cup red wine		

Cook the pasta according to package directions. Remove with tongs and drain, saving the cooking water. Rinse under cold water.

Add the potatoes to the pasta water and cook over medium-high heat for 15 minutes, or until tender. Drain the potatoes and place in a large bowl. Using a fork or potato masher, coarsely mash the potatoes.

Meanwhile, heat the oil in a large skillet over medium-low heat. Add the onion and cook for 15 minutes, or until very soft and golden brown. Add the garlic, oregano, and wine and continue cooking for 5 minutes, or until the wine is reduced by half. Add the spinach, cover, and cook for 3 minutes, or until wilted.

Break the cheese into small pieces and add with the potatoes to the pan with the spinach mixture, tossing until well-blended. Season with salt and pepper to taste.

Preheat the oven to 375°F.

Pour one-third of the pasta sauce in the bottom of a 13" × 9" baking dish. Evenly divide the spinach mixture among the shells and place them on top of the sauce. Pour the remaining sauce over all. Bake for 35 minutes, or until warm and bubbly. Garnish with the parsley.

Makes 6 servings

Per serving: 406 calories, 16 g protein, 42 g carbohydrates, 19 g fat, 27 mg cholesterol, 5 g fiber, 714 g sodium

POTATO SALAD WITH ANCHOVIES AND CAPERS

3   tablespoons olive oil

3   tablespoons red wine vinegar

3   tablespoons grated red onion

1   tablespoon Dijon mustard

1   tablespoon sugar

¼   teaspoon salt

½   teaspoon freshly ground black pepper or to taste

2   pounds boiling potatoes

3   celery ribs, thinly sliced

2   green onions, thinly sliced

4   hard-cooked eggs, peeled and chopped

1   can (2 ounces) anchovies, drained and chopped (optional)

2   tablespoons capers, drained

½   cup sour cream or plain yogurt

Premixing the first seven ingredients and letting them marinate for a while is the key to the success of this recipe. If anchovies aren't your thing, omit them; the salad will still be full-bodied.

In a medium bowl, whisk together the oil, vinegar, red onion, mustard, sugar, salt, and pepper. Allow to stand at room temperature for 30 minutes.

Meanwhile, bring a large pot of salted water to a boil over medium-high heat. Cook the potatoes whole and unpeeled for 15 minutes, or until tender. Drain and rinse under cold water. If desired, slip off the potato skins. Cut the potatoes into bite-size pieces.

Add the potatoes, celery, green onions, eggs, anchovies (if using), capers, and sour cream or yogurt to the bowl with the vinaigrette. Toss to coat well.

Makes 8 servings

Per serving: 220 calories, 8 g protein, 26 g carbohydrates, 10 g fat, 115 mg cholesterol, 2 g fiber, 682 mg sodium

I have taught my boys that there are a handful of recipes that they need to know in order to cook and wow others with homemade cooking. Besides pie crust, ricotta gnocchi, and homemade meat loaf, this basic vinaigrette is on the top of the list.

THE WORLD'S EASIEST VINAIGRETTE

2   garlic cloves, minced

¼   cup vinegar (such as balsamic, rice wine, raspberry, or sherry wine vinegar)

½   teaspoon salt

¼   teaspoon freshly ground black pepper

½   cup extra virgin olive oil

In a small bowl, combine the garlic, vinegar, salt, and pepper. Whisk in the oil until well-blended.

Makes 6 servings

Per serving: 174 calories, 0 g protein, 3 g carbohydrates, 18 g fat, 0 mg cholesterol, 0 g fiber, 196 mg sodium

KITCHEN TIP

Once you have the basic recipe, experiment with variations by adding different herbs, spices, or condiments. Here are a few of my favorite combinations.

Asian: Omit the salt, add 2 tablespoons soy sauce or tamari, 1 tablespoon grated fresh ginger, and 1 teaspoon toasted sesame oil.

Creamy Blue: Add 4 tablespoons sour cream or plain yogurt and 4 ounces blue cheese or Gorgonzola cheese, crumbled.

Honey-Mustard: Add 2 tablespoons honey and 1 tablespoon Dijon mustard.

GORGONZOLA POTATOES AND PEAS

1½	pounds small red potatoes	4	ounces Gorgonzola cheese, crumbled
1	pound whole peas, shelled, or 1 cup frozen peas, thawed	3	tablespoons chopped fresh chives
4	tablespoons butter	½	teaspoon freshly grated nutmeg
4	tablespoons unbleached all-purpose flour	¼	teaspoon white pepper
2	cups milk		

Bring a large pot of salted water to a boil over medium-high heat. Cook the potatoes whole and unpeeled for 15 minutes, or until tender, adding the peas during the last 3 minutes of cooking time. Drain. Leaving the skin on the potatoes, cut into quarters.

Preheat the oven to 400°F. Lightly butter a 2-quart baking dish.

Melt the butter in a large saucepan over medium heat. Whisk in the flour and cook until the flour turns a light brown. Very gradually whisk in the milk. Cook for 5 minutes, or until the sauce simmers and thickens. Stir in the cheese, chives, nutmeg, and pepper. Add the potatoes and peas and toss to coat well.

Pour into the prepared baking dish. Bake for 30 minutes, or until heated through and lightly browned.

Makes 8 servings

Per serving: 243 calories, 8 g protein, 26 g carbohydrates, 12 g fat, 36 mg cholesterol, 2 g fiber, 95 mg sodium

I am one of those people who skips dessert but overindulges in creamy rich dishes like this one. Even though potatoes and pasta may not seem impressive, this recipe tossed with egg noodles is heavenly and oh, so decadent.

This creamy rice dish is inarguably delicious. I particularly like it as a bed for grilled salmon.

ASPARAGUS AND BRIE RISOTTO

4	cups vegetable or chicken broth	1	pound asparagus, trimmed and cut into 2" pieces
2	tablespoons olive oil	½	teaspoon freshly ground black pepper
4	green onions, minced		
1	cup Arborio rice	6	ounces Brie cheese, cubed

Bring the broth to a boil in a large saucepan over medium heat. Reduce the heat to low, cover, and simmer.

Heat the oil in a deep heavy saucepan over medium heat. Add the green onions and rice and cook for 5 minutes, or until the rice is golden brown. Begin adding the broth, ½ cup at a time, and cook, stirring constantly, for 20 minutes, or until the broth is absorbed and the risotto begins to get creamy. Just before adding the last amount of broth, add the asparagus and pepper.

Stir in the cheese.

Makes 4 servings

Per serving: 362 calories, 17 g protein, 46 g carbohydrates, 15 g fat, 28 mg cholesterol, 4 g fiber, 851 mg sodium

Sometimes the simplest dishes are the most memorable. Spring onions are delicate, and this lovely way of serving them brings forth the sweetness.

KITCHEN TIP

For a richer version of this dish, after reducing the cooking liquid, add ¼ cup heavy cream.

SPRING ONIONS AMANDINE

1	cup chicken or vegetable broth	½	cup whole natural almonds, coarsely chopped
1	pound small-bulb spring or pearl onions	1	tablespoon chopped fresh dill
¼	teaspoon saffron threads (optional)	¼	teaspoon salt
1½	tablespoons unsalted butter	⅛	teaspoon freshly ground black pepper

In a medium saucepan over high heat, bring the broth, onions, and saffron (if using) to a boil. Reduce the heat to medium-low, cover, and simmer for 20 minutes, or until the onions are tender. Remove from the heat. Using a slotted spoon, remove the onions to a bowl and keep warm.

Return the pan to the heat and cook the liquid over high heat for 4 minutes, or until reduced to ¼ cup. Add the butter, almonds, dill, salt, and pepper and cook for 1 minute. Return the onions to the mixture and cook for 2 minutes longer, or until heated through.

Makes 6 servings

Per serving: 166 calories, 7 g protein, 7 g carbohydrates, 13 g fat, 8 mg cholesterol, 3 g fiber, 224 mg sodium

CREAMY NOODLES WITH LEEKS AND PEAS

12	ounces egg noodles	2	tablespoons butter
1	cup fresh or frozen peas	2	tablespoons chopped fresh dill
1½	cups vegetable or chicken broth	2	tablespoons chopped fresh chives
2	pounds baby or small leeks, sliced (see tip)		Salt
1½	cups cottage cheese		Freshly ground black pepper

Cook the noodles according to package directions. Add the peas during the last 2 minutes of cooking.

Meanwhile, in a medium skillet over medium heat, bring the broth to a simmer and add the leeks. Reduce the heat to low, cover, and simmer for 5 to 7 minutes, or until the leeks are very soft. Remove with a slotted spoon and place in a large serving bowl. Reserve the broth.

Drain the noodles and peas and add to the bowl with the leeks. Add the cottage cheese, butter, dill, and chives. Stir until well-blended. Season with salt and pepper to taste.

If the noodles are not moist enough for your taste, add a few tablespoons of the reserved broth.

Makes 6 servings

Per serving: 421 calories, 19 g protein, 67 g carbohydrates, 9 g fat, 73 mg cholesterol, 6 g fiber, 408 mg sodium

I am an old-fashioned girl who still enjoys the pleasures of simple, uncomplicated dishes. This recipe exemplifies this. It is outstanding as an accompaniment for meat and poultry. But very often, I find myself eating only a few bites of meat and instead reaching for seconds of these wonderful noodles, enjoying them more as an entrée.

KITCHEN TIP

Leeks are a dirty crop. A bit of the growing soil is usually found between the layers. The best way to clean them is to cut them in half lengthwise, then crosswise into ½" slices. Soak in a large bowl of water for 5 minutes, stirring occasionally to dislodge the dirt, letting it settle to the bottom of the bowl. Remove them with a slotted spoon to a colander and rinse and drain.

KITCHEN TIP

For an extra-spectacular dessert, glaze the cake with a combination of 1 cup confectioner's sugar, 1 teaspoon pure vanilla extract, and 1 to 2 tablespoons milk. Add the milk gradually until it's a spreading consistency. Glaze the cake and garnish with additional organic rose petals.

HERB GARDEN ANGEL FOOD CAKE

1 cup sifted cake flour	1½ teaspoons cream of tartar
½ cup sifted confectioners' sugar	1 teaspoon vanilla extract
¼ teaspoon salt	1 cup granulated sugar
1½ cups egg whites (about 12 large eggs), at room temperature	3 tablespoons chopped purple basil or regular basil
	1 cup chopped organically grown rose petals

Preheat the oven to 350°F.

In a medium bowl, combine the flour, confectioners' sugar, and salt.

In a large bowl with an electric mixer on high speed, beat the egg whites and cream of tartar until frothy. Add the vanilla extract and beat until soft peaks form. Gradually beat in the granulated sugar, ¼ cup at a time, until glossy, stiff peaks form and the sugar dissolves. (To be sure that the sugar has dissolved, rub the beaten whites between your fingers. They should not feel granular.)

Gently fold the flour mixture into the egg white mixture in 4 stages. When the last bit of flour mixture is to be folded in, add the basil and rose petals.

Gently pour the batter into an ungreased 10" tube pan. Bake for 45 minutes, or until the top is golden brown and a wooden pick inserted in the center comes out clean. Remove from the oven and invert, allowing to cool completely in the pan. When the cake is cool, run a thin knife between the cake and the pan. Turn out onto a plate.

Makes 8 servings
Per serving: 193 calories, 6 g protein, 42 g carbohydrates, 0 g fat, 0 mg cholesterol, 0 g fiber, 148 mg sodium

I find this cake somewhat whimsical—a simple spice cake studded with juicy blackberries. Serve it warm with vanilla ice cream or slightly sweetened whipped cream.

KITCHEN TIP

You can substitute frozen berries for the fresh ones. Instead of mixing them into the batter, scatter them on the bottom of the pan before baking. When you invert the pan, the juices will act like a glaze.

BLACKBERRY SPICE CAKE

2	large eggs	1	teaspoon ground ginger
⅓	cup vegetable oil	1	teaspoon baking powder
1	cup vanilla yogurt	¾	teaspoon ground allspice
1	cup packed brown sugar	½	teaspoon freshly grated nutmeg
1½	cups whole grain pastry flour	½	teaspoon baking soda
1½	teaspoons ground cinnamon	½	teaspoon salt
		2	cups blackberries

Preheat the oven to 350°F. Lightly oil a 9" cake pan.

In a medium bowl, combine the eggs, oil, and yogurt. Stir in the brown sugar.

In a large bowl, combine the flour, cinnamon, ginger, baking powder, allspice, nutmeg, baking soda, and salt. Form a well in the center and add the yogurt mixture, stirring just until blended. Fold in the blackberries.

Pour the batter into the prepared pan and bake for 50 to 55 minutes, or until a wooden pick inserted in the center comes out clean. Cool on a rack for 5 minutes. Run a knife around the inside of the pan and tap it on all sides to loosen. Invert onto a serving plate.

Makes 8 servings
Per serving: 342 calories, 6 g protein, 56 g carbohydrates, 11 g fat, 55 mg cholesterol, 2 g fiber, 240 mg sodium

CHOCOLATE RICE PUDDING WITH RASPBERRY SAUCE

2	cups half-and-half		1	teaspoon vanilla extract
4	ounces sweetened dark chocolate, chopped		2	eggs, beaten
1½	cups cooked rice		½	pint raspberries
¾	cup + 2 tablespoons sugar		1	tablespoon balsamic vinegar
1	teaspoon ground cinnamon			

Preheat the oven to 350°F. Fill a large baking pan with 2 cups water. Have a 1½-quart baking dish ready but do not grease it.

In a medium saucepan over medium heat, cook the half-and-half and chocolate, stirring, for 3 minutes, or until the chocolate is melted.

In a medium bowl, combine the rice, ¾ cup of the sugar, cinnamon, vanilla extract, and eggs. Whisk the half-and-half mixture into the rice mixture.

Pour into the baking dish and place the baking dish in the pan with the water. Bake for 50 to 60 minutes, or until a knife inserted in the center comes out clean.

Meanwhile, place the berries in a food processor or blender. Process until smooth. Place in a small bowl with the remaining 2 tablespoons sugar and vinegar. Serve the sauce over the pudding.

Makes 10 servings

Per serving: 244 calories, 4 g protein, 35 g carbohydrates, 11 g fat, 60 mg cholesterol, 2 g fiber, 35 mg sodium

Rice pudding is one of my favorite desserts. It takes me back to the nights when my dad would make me a snack of milk and rice with a little sugar and vanilla. My love for rice pudding led me to this wonderful, rich, uncomplicated way of taking something humble and making it extraordinary. It's a great way to use up leftover rice as well.

HORIZON ORGANIC DAIRY

Although Horizon Organic Dairy doesn't claim that its Happy Cows™ are sacred, the nation's leading organic dairy treats its most honored employees like deities.

The cows are milked three times a day to prevent painful milk buildup, with pneumatic milking machines specially designed to increase comfort. The animals are fed a diet of certified organic hay, oats, canola, and other organic grains that are carefully balanced by Horizon's own animal nutritionist.

Since this organically raised "cow chow" contains no chemical contaminants, neither does Bessie's moo juice. Consumers swear that Horizon Organic™ stands head and shoulders above the milk from those other farms.

Horizon farmers are sticklers about well-cow care. Keeping the Happy Cows™ healthy in the first place just makes good sense. That way, the organic farmers rely on preventive care instead of drugs to keep cows healthy. You see, cows are creatures of habit and don't like changes in routine, excess noise, or inferior feed. If a cow does get sick, she's nursed back to health with aspirin, massage, and other natural treatments. In the event that a cow does not respond, the animal is removed from the herd permanently and is treated and sold.

The Horizon farmers have also found that letting Mother Nature take her course works more efficiently than artificial insemination.

Arnold Tebbetts, a small family farmer near Montpelier, Vermont, supplies milk for the Organic Cow brand, a sister brand under the Horizon Organic umbrella.

David W. Harp/Horizon

About once a year, each cow gets a date with a live bull.

Horizon spells out its philosophy in an annual report that proudly displays its flying Happy Cow logo. The company believes that food can and should be produced in harmony with nature and that animals used for food production should be raised and nurtured with respect for their natural patterns.

The "cowboys" behind Horizon, Paul Repetto and Mark Retzloff, teamed up in 1991 in Boulder, Colorado. As natural-foods veterans, they were dismayed by the lack of organic dairy foods in the marketplace. So they filled the void, first with certified organic yogurt, then with certified organic milk.

Little Number One was the first calf born on the Horizon Organic farm in Chestertown, Maryland.

Their timing was perfect.

In 1993, the Food and Drug Administration gave dairy farmers the go-ahead to use the genetically engineered bovine growth hormone (rBGH) to increase cows' milk output. Consumer and animal-rights activists, as well as agricultural experts, raised such a ruckus that rBGH was banned in Europe and Canada. In the United States, demand for hormone-free milk skyrocketed.

Today, Horizon has milked the competition to become the nation's largest organic-milk producer. It's also the nation's only milk producer—organic or conventional—that distributes fresh, fluid milk in all 50 states.

The company markets nearly 100 different organic products, including chocolate milk, cheese, and low-fat yogurt, in all sizes of containers. The logo showing the Happy Cow flying over the Earth has become so recognizable that it's even found on the company's nondairy products, including a line of organic fruit juices and organic eggs.

But Horizon's heart will always be down on the dairy farm.

About half of the organic company's milk comes from organic farms that it owns in Idaho and Maryland. The other half comes from smaller, independent organic dairy farms scattered throughout the country. All must adhere to Horizon's strict standards.

Farmers can feed their cows only hay and grain grown on land that has been free of synthetic pesticides, herbicides, and fertilizers for at least 3 years. Cows must be on this diet for at least 1 year before their milk can be sold to Horizon.

With Horizon-brand products moving quickly off the shelves, it seems certain that organic dairy foods will grow in popularity as more consumers vote for healthier foods for themselves and for their families.

EARLY SUMMER

June 21, the first day of summer, signals the moment when the cooks in my kitchen at Flea St. Café start pleading for fresh tomatoes. After being deprived of sun-ripened tomatoes since mid-October, their patience has disappeared. Whether the early summer is warm or not, they want—even demand—tomatoes, symbols of the start of consistently warmer days. With the influence of Mediterranean cooking in our cuisine, tomatoes, as well as other summer vegetables, play integral roles in our entrées.

But early summer is just that—early. The curtain of sunshine is only beginning to be pulled back to spotlight the harvesting of spring crops. It is a time of tiny but tasty foods. The tomatoes that we use during this season are cherry tomatoes, pint-size and delectably sweet. They make their way into salads, quick sauces, and sandwiches.

Mushrooms, herbs, potatoes, onions, squash blossoms, early eggplant, and peppers are also available during this time. Stone fruits such as peaches,

cherries, and apricots as well as blueberries and strawberries are in abundance and at their tastiest. Fruits are used frequently in savory and sweet dishes. To support your organic kitchen, use this time to freeze as many fruits as possible for use later in the year.

My cooking takes its cue from the weather shifts common in early summer. As you will notice, this chapter offers quick, easy, and light recipes as well as those that take more time and warm up the kitchen.

The real heat of summer is just around the corner.

KITCHEN TIPS

When purchasing scallops, look for day boat ones. These are naturally harvested and not treated with bleaches or chemicals. Because of this, the scallops are often different sizes and range from light pink to pale gray in color. They taste just as delicious and are much healthier.

I like to serve the cakes with a homemade tartar sauce made from mayonnaise, relish, capers, and grated red onion.

SALMON AND SCALLOP CAKES

¾	pound salmon fillet, skinned and boned	2	teaspoons Worcestershire sauce
¼	pound sea scallops (see tip)	1	egg
	Pinch + ⅛ teaspoon salt	3	green onions, thinly sliced
	Freshly ground black pepper	1	tablespoon chopped fresh dill
½	cup dried bread crumbs	⅓	cup cornmeal
½	cup mayonnaise	⅛	teaspoon ground red pepper (optional)
1	tablespoon Dijon mustard	3	tablespoons olive oil

Preheat the oven to 400°F. Lightly season the salmon and scallops with a pinch of salt and black pepper to taste. Place on a large baking pan and bake for 10 minutes, or until just opaque. Remove from the oven and cool slightly, but don't turn off the oven. Wipe the baking pan clean.

Meanwhile, in a large bowl, combine the bread crumbs, mayonnaise, mustard, Worcestershire sauce, egg, onions, and dill. Crumble the salmon and finely chop the scallops and add to the bowl, tossing until well-blended. Form into 8 large or 16 small cakes.

In a pie plate, combine the cornmeal, the remaining ⅛ teaspoon salt, and red pepper, if using. Thoroughly coat the cakes with the cornmeal mixture. Place on the baking pan. Brush with half the oil and turn. Brush with the remaining oil.

For larger cakes, bake for 15 to 18 minutes, turning once, until browned. Bake smaller cakes for 10 to 12 minutes.

Makes 8 servings

Per serving: 268 calories, 13 g protein, 10 g carbohydrates, 19 g fat, 61 mg cholesterol, 1 g fiber, 298 mg sodium

I like this appetizer because it is not only beautiful but also a light, fresh start to a meal. Both the beans and tomatoes need to be in small pieces to avoid too much mess. There are some great organic beers on the market, which I think are a perfect match for this dish.

SUMMER BEAN AND TOMATOES BRUSCHETTA

½ pint miniature or cherry tomatoes, cut in half or quarters

½ small red onion, thinly sliced

1 garlic clove, minced

¼ cup finely sliced fresh basil

3 tablespoons extra virgin olive oil

2 tablespoons balsamic vinegar

½ teaspoon salt

⅛ pound small green or wax beans, diagonally cut into ½" pieces

12 thick diagonal slices whole grain or hearty Italian bread

6 ounces soft goat cheese (such as chèvre)

Freshly ground black pepper

Preheat the broiler. Bring a medium pot of water to a boil over high heat.

In a large bowl, combine the tomatoes, onion, garlic, basil, oil, vinegar, and salt. Toss to coat well. Let stand for at least 15 minutes.

Meanwhile, add the beans to the boiling water and cook for 3 minutes, or until tender-crisp. Drain and rinse with cold water. Add to tomato mixture.

Place the bread slices on the broiler pan. Broil for 2 minutes, or until lightly browned. Turn the slices and brush each with some of the juices from the marinated tomatoes. Broil for 2 minutes longer, or until browned.

Remove the bread and place on a large serving platter, moistened side up. Evenly divide the cheese among the bread slices and spread over each.

Evenly divide the tomato mixture over the cheese and sprinkle with pepper to taste.

Makes 12 servings

Per serving: 155 calories, 6 g protein, 17 g carbohydrates, 8 g fat, 7 mg cholesterol, 3 g fiber, 288 mg sodium

SUMMER STRATA

2	tablespoons extra virgin olive oil	¾	teaspoon salt
2	medium zucchini and/or yellow squash, thinly sliced	¼	teaspoon black pepper
		1	loaf challah or sweet Italian bread, broken into bite-size pieces
1	red onion, thinly sliced		
2	garlic cloves, minced		
12	eggs	8	ounces soft goat cheese (such as chèvre or brie), broken into small pieces
2	cups whole milk		
½	cup chopped fresh basil		
2	tablespoons chopped fresh oregano	⅓	cup sliced pitted green olives
1	cup unbleached all-purpose flour	½	cup (2 ounces) grated Asiago or Parmesan cheese

Preheat the oven to 350°F. Lightly oil a 13" × 9" baking dish.

Heat the oil in a large skillet over medium-high heat. Add the zucchini or yellow squash and onion and cook for 4 minutes, or until slightly softened. Remove from the heat and stir in the garlic. Drain off any liquid. Set aside to cool to room temperature.

In a medium bowl, whisk together the eggs, milk, basil, and oregano. Gradually whisk in the flour, salt, and pepper.

Place the bread in the prepared baking dish. Top with half of the zucchini mixture. Dollop half of the goat cheese and olives on top of the vegetables. Pour the egg mixture over the bread and vegetables. Top with the remaining vegetables, goat cheese, and olives and press them gently into the egg mixture. Sprinkle with the grated cheese.

Bake for 45 minutes, or until a knife inserted into the center comes out clean. Let stand for 10 minutes before cutting. Serve warm or at room temperature.

Makes 12 servings

Per serving: 327 calories, 17 g protein, 29 g carbohydrates, 16 g fat, 230 mg cholesterol, 1 g fiber, 641 mg sodium

If you can, use both zucchini and yellow squash in this wonderful summery dish. Delicious as a first course, the strata is also a wonderful addition to a brunch buffet. The recipe calls for readily available Italian bread, but if you can, use brioche or challah instead.

KITCHEN TIP

Make this dish year-round using the most seasonal vegetables at the time. Vary the cheese as well. For the fall, try broccoli, cauliflower, and Cheddar. In the spring, use sliced snow peas and baby carrots with Jarlsberg cheese.

This savory dish is like a bean stew. The corn relish is a wonderful way to showcase the first-of-the-season fresh corn, but it's equally good with frozen corn. Serve with warm corn tortillas and top the beans with a big dollop of sour cream.

BLACK BEANS WITH CORN RELISH

Beans

2	tablespoons olive oil		8	ounces extra-firm tofu (regular or smoked), drained and cubed
1	onion, chopped			
1	carrot, thinly sliced		1	cup vegetable broth
1	celery rib, thinly sliced		1	teaspoon ground cumin
2	garlic cloves, minced		1½	teaspoons chili powder
⅓	cup chopped fresh jicama (½ of a small one)		2	tablespoons chopped fresh oregano
3	cups cooked black beans		1	teaspoon salt

Corn Relish

1½	cups fresh or frozen corn kernels		½	teaspoon red-pepper flakes (or chopped chile peppers to taste)
1	garlic clove, minced			
2	green onions, thinly sliced		1½	teaspoons ground cumin
3	tablespoons chopped fresh basil		1½	tablespoons brown sugar
	Juice of 1 lime		½	teaspoon salt

To make the beans: Heat the oil in a large skillet over medium heat. Add the onion, carrot, celery, garlic, and jicama and cook for 4 minutes, or until slightly softened. Add the beans, tofu, broth, cumin, chili powder, oregano, and salt. Bring to a boil. Reduce the heat to low, cover, and simmer, stirring occasionally, for 30 minutes.

To make the corn relish: Meanwhile, bring a small pot of water to a boil over high heat. Blanch the corn in the water for 3 minutes. Drain and immediately pour the corn into an ice bath to cool. Drain and place in a medium bowl. Add the garlic, green onions, basil, lime juice, red-pepper flakes or chile peppers, cumin, brown sugar, and salt.

To serve, evenly divide the bean mixture among 4 bowls and top with the corn relish.

Makes 4 servings
Per serving: 315 calories, 19 g protein, 40 g carbohydrates, 11 g fat, 0 mg cholesterol, 14 g fiber, 790 mg sodium

LAMB CHOPS WITH TOMATO SALSA

- 8 lamb rib or loin chops
- 2 tablespoons olive oil
- 2 garlic cloves, minced
- 1 tablespoon minced fresh rosemary
- ½ teaspoon salt
- ½ teaspoon freshly ground black pepper
- ½ pint cherry tomatoes, halved
- 2 tablespoons grated red onion
- 3 tablespoons chopped fresh mint
- Juice of 1 lime
- ½ teaspoon ground cumin
- ½ teaspoon chili powder
- 1 teaspoon sugar
- 1 avocado, peeled, pitted, and cut into bite-size pieces

Heat the broiler or grill. Place the lamb in a medium bowl and add the oil, garlic, rosemary, salt, and pepper. Toss to coat. Let stand for 10 minutes.

In another medium bowl, combine the tomatoes, onion, mint, lime juice, cumin, chili powder, sugar, and avocado.

Broil or grill the chops for 5 minutes, turning once, until browned and a thermometer inserted in the center registers 145°F for medium-rare.

Place the chops on plates and top generously with the salsa.

Makes 4 servings

Per serving: 425 calories, 33 g protein, 9 g carbohydrates, 28 g fat, 103 mg cholesterol, 7 g fiber, 114 mg sodium

There are a handful of organic lamb companies around the country, and the lamb they produce is wonderful. I like lamb chops on the bone, emphatic that anyone who doesn't pick them up with their fingers, enjoying every morsel, is missing out on the best part.

KITCHEN TIP

Because the first tomatoes of the season are cherries, I use them in this recipe. Later in the season, I use cut-up big tomatoes and, when possible, a whole variety of colors.

HERB AND FLOWER–CRUSTED HALIBUT

½ cup chopped fresh parsley

4 tablespoons chopped organically grown edible flower petals (such as calendula, nasturtiums, roses, onion, or chive blossoms)

2 tablespoons chopped fresh chives

2 tablespoons chopped fresh basil

1 tablespoon chopped fresh oregano

½ teaspoon salt

¼ teaspoon freshly ground black pepper

1½ pounds halibut fillet, cut into 4 pieces

2 tablespoons olive oil

1 cup chicken, vegetable, or fish broth

¼ teaspoon saffron

2 garlic cloves, minced

1 cup fresh or thawed frozen peas

In a shallow bowl, combine the parsley, flower petals, chives, basil, oregano, salt, and pepper.

Place the halibut in the herb mixture, pressing the fish to thoroughly coat both sides. Set aside.

Heat the oil in a large skillet over medium-high heat. Add the halibut and cook for 4 minutes. Turn the halibut and pour in the broth. Add the saffron and garlic. Simmer for 5 minutes, or until the halibut is just opaque and the broth is reduced by half. During the last minute or so, add the peas.

Remove the pan from the heat. Place 1 fish fillet in each of 4 shallow soup bowls. Evenly divide the broth and peas among the bowls.

Makes 4 servings

Per serving: 287 calories, 38 g protein, 7 g carbohydrates, 11 g fat, 54 mg cholesterol, 2 g fiber, 241 mg sodium

The herbs and blossoms on this fish not only look spectacular but they also add a summery flavor to the light broth and peas beneath the fish. At Flea St. Café, we serve it over buttermilk mashed potatoes, which is heavenly.

KITCHEN TIPS

Substitute salmon or any mild, firm fish fillet for the halibut.

Whenever possible, try to buy line-caught and wild fish.

Courtesy of Frontera Grill

Rick Bayless

Frontera Grill and *Topolobampo*, Chicago

Food is only as healthy as the earth it springs from. Good food is what nourishes great civilizations. It connects body and spirit, and it connects humans to the earth that sustains them.

LAMB BARBACOA

3   medium red potatoes, cut into ½" dice

2   medium carrots, cut into ½" dice

1   medium white onion, halved and sliced

2   garlic cloves, halved

1   cup cooked (or canned) garbanzo beans

1   large sprig of epazote (if you can find it)

1   3-pound rolled and tied boneless lamb shoulder roast

¾   teaspoon salt, preferably coarse, plus some for sprinkling on lamb

3   tablespoons chopped fresh cilantro

1   canned chipotle chile en adobo, seeded and finely chopped

1½   cups salsa (such as Essential Roasted Tomatillo-Chipotle Salsa)

2   tablespoons finely crumbled Mexican queso añejo or Parmesan

1   cup good quality manzanillo olives, pitted

16   large (10") flour tortillas, warmed

About 30 minutes before cooking, prepare a charcoal fire, letting the coals burn until they are covered with a gray ash and are medium-hot. Bank the coals on two sides of the lower grate to prepare for the indirect cooking that follows.

In a 12" × 9" heavy-duty aluminum-foil pan, combine the potatoes, carrots, onion, garlic, garbanzos, and epazote. Position the pan in the center of the lower grate and surround with the coals. Pour water into the pan to about 1" from the top (it'll take about 5 cups). Position the cooking grate 8" above the coals and set an oven thermometer on it, if you have one.

Sprinkle the lamb liberally with salt. Lay the roast in the center of the cooking grate directly over the soup, cover the grill, and cook, maintaining a moderately low temperature (between 250° and 300°F), checking every 30 minutes, and adding coals as needed. The lamb will be beautifully smoky-roasted—it'll register about 170°F on a meat thermometer

and be very tender in about 2½ hours. Be sure to check periodically the slow-simmering soup to ensure the liquid level remains more or less the same, adding more water if it's needed.

Remove the roast to a platter. Sprinkle with the salt and let rest, covered, for about 20 minutes.

Meanwhile, with the precision of a steady-handed circus performer, carefully remove the pan of soup from the bottom of the grill. Skim off the fat, then taste and season with salt, usually about ¾ teaspoon. Stir in the cilantro and chipotle and ladle into small soup cups.

Place the salsa in a bowl and sprinkle with cheese. Remove the strings from the lamb. Slice into good, thick slabs and arrange on a warm platter. Strew the olives around the platter and carry to the table with a flourish. Serve each guest a cup of soup, and pass the meat, salsa, and the warm tortillas for everyone to make delicious soft tacos.

Makes 8 servings

PENNE WITH STUFFED MEATBALLS

1½ pounds ground beef, chicken, or turkey

1 small onion, grated

3 slices white bread, broken into small pieces

¼ cup milk

1 egg, beaten

½ teaspoon salt

¼ teaspoon freshly ground black pepper

¼ cup chopped fresh parsley

8 ounces mozzarella cheese, cut into 24 squares

2 tablespoons olive oil

2 large leeks, whites only, sliced and washed thoroughly

2 garlic cloves, minced

8 cups chopped seeded tomatoes (about 8)

1 cup chopped fresh basil

3 tablespoons chopped fresh oregano

½ cup red wine (optional)

12 ounces penne pasta

¼ cup (1 ounce) grated or shaved Italian cheese (such as Parmesan, Asiago, or Romano)

In a large bowl, combine the meat with the onion, bread, milk, egg, salt, pepper, and parsley. Blend well using your hands. Divide the meat mixture into 24 portions and wrap each around a cube of mozzarella, completely surrounding it. Be sure that there are no leaks, or the mozzarella will ooze into the sauce.

Heat the oil in a large sauce pot over medium-high heat. Brown the meatballs carefully on all sides. Remove to a bowl. Add the leeks and garlic to the pot and cook for 5 minutes, or until softened. Add the tomatoes, basil, oregano, and wine, if using, and bring to a boil. Reduce the heat to low and simmer for 10 minutes.

Meanwhile, cook the pasta according to package directions. Drain and place in a large serving bowl or platter. Top with the meatballs and the sauce. Garnish with the grated cheese.

Makes 8 servings

Per serving: 781 calories, 44 g protein, 72 g carbohydrates, 34 g fat, 136 mg cholesterol, 6 g fiber, 563 mg sodium

There is something kidlike about meatballs, especially these with the added surprise of melted mozzarella oozing out.

KITCHEN TIP

When fresh tomatoes aren't in season, substitute organic canned tomatoes.

I like to roast a chicken whole. I think the meat stays moister, and I just like the way it looks when served. There are a growing number of organic chicken farms all over the country. I'm often asked what makes a chicken organic. The simple answer is that the chicken is fed all organic feed and not injected with hormones or given unneccessary antibiotics.

ROASTED CHICKEN AND PEACHES

1	teaspoon salt	6	peaches, pitted and quartered
½	teaspoon freshly ground black pepper	½	teaspoon freshly grated nutmeg
1	teaspoon ground cumin		
1	whole chicken (about 3 pounds)	1	teaspoon ground cinnamon
1½	teaspoons olive oil	2	tablespoons chopped fresh tarragon
4	leeks, white and light green parts, thinly sliced and washed thoroughly	3	tablespoons brown sugar

Preheat the oven to 400°F.

In a small bowl, combine the salt, pepper, and cumin.

Rub the chicken with the oil and season generously with the cumin mixture. Place the chicken in a roasting pan.

In a large bowl, combine the leeks, peaches, nutmeg, cinnamon, tarragon, and brown sugar. Scatter the mixture around the bottom of the chicken in the pan. Roast the chicken for 30 minutes. Stir the peaches occasionally to coat with the pan juices. Reduce the heat to 350°F and cook for 30 minutes, or until a thermometer inserted in a breast registers 180°F and the juices run clear. Let stand for 10 minutes before carving.

Remove from the oven and place the chicken on a platter, either whole or cut into pieces. Pour the pan juices, leeks, and peaches over all.

Makes 6 servings

Per serving: 502 calories, 51 g protein, 23 g carbohydrates, 22 g fat, 146 mg cholesterol, 3 g fiber, 679 mg sodium

STEAK WITH FRUIT SAUCE

½ pint red raspberries

3 tablespoons sugar

2 tablespoons balsamic vinegar

1 tablespoon olive oil

1 small red onion, thinly sliced

8 large or 16 small figs, quartered

2 ounces ham, chopped

1 teaspoon finely chopped fresh rosemary

¾ teaspoon garam masala

Freshly ground black pepper

8 boneless rib-eye or beef tenderloin steaks (about 2½ pounds)

Salt

6 ounces blue cheese, crumbled

Preheat the grill or broiler. Lightly oil the grill rack or broiler pan.

In a small saucepan over medium heat, combine the raspberries, sugar, and vinegar. Simmer for 10 minutes, or until reduced by half. Set aside.

Meanwhile, heat the oil in a medium skillet over medium heat. Add the onion and cook for 5 minutes, or until soft. Add the figs, ham, rosemary, garam masala, and ½ teaspoon pepper. Cook for 5 minutes, or until the figs are very soft. Set aside and keep warm.

Season the steaks generously with salt and pepper. Grill or broil the steaks for 12 minutes, turning once, until a thermometer inserted in the center registers 145°F for medium-rare.

Place each steak on a plate. Evenly divide the cheese on top of the steaks and cover with some of the fig mixture. Drizzle a few tablespoons of the raspberry sauce over all. Serve the remaining fig mixture on the side.

Makes 8 servings

Per serving: 277 calories, 19 g protein, 21 g carbohydrates, 13 g fat, 47 mg cholesterol, 4 g fiber, 432 mg sodium

My dad had a grocery store, and my uncle owned the local meat-processing plant. They sold both kosher and naturally prepared meats. So even before I knew it, the meat that my family ate was as close to organic as you could find in those days. The combination of the figs, blue cheese, and balsamic raspberry sauce is divine over steak.

KITCHEN TIP

These days, there are more options to find well-raised cattle, which are freely grazed, free of growth hormones and antibiotics, and treated humanely. If you can find organic meat, always opt for it. Natural meat is the next best thing and would make the best second choice. I even buy frozen meat if it is organic. It's worth the extra money.

KITCHEN TIP

I love to share my chutney with my neighbors and friends. For a decorative presentation, wrap some fabric or twine around the jar. There is nothing that compares with a gift of something homemade from your kitchen.

APRICOT-CHERRY CHUTNEY

2	cups sliced seeded apricots (about 6 large)		1	cup cider vinegar
2	cups pitted cherries or blueberries		2	cinnamon sticks
1	large onion, thinly sliced		¼	cup chopped fresh ginger
2	cups packed brown sugar		2	teaspoons red-pepper flakes (optional)
			2	teaspoons salt

In a large saucepan, combine the apricots, cherries or blueberries, onion, brown sugar, vinegar, cinnamon sticks, ginger, red-pepper flakes (if using), and salt. Bring to a boil over medium-high heat. Reduce the heat to low and simmer, stirring occasionally, for 1½ hours, or until thickened. Remove from the heat and cool to room temperature. Remove and discard the cinnamon sticks.

Place the chutney in five ½-pint containers. Refrigerate for up to 1 month.

Makes 2½ pints

Per 2 tablespoons: 39 calories, 0 g protein, 10 g carbohydrates, 0 g fat, 0 mg cholesterol, 1 g fiber, 119 mg sodium

CUCUMBER AND LAVENDER SALAD

1   large cucumber, very thinly sliced

1   red onion, thinly sliced

½   red bell pepper, thinly sliced

¼   cup seasoned rice wine vinegar

2   tablespoons extra virgin olive oil

1   tablespoon chopped fresh lavender

1   garlic clove, minced

½   teaspoon salt

¼   teaspoon freshly ground black pepper

In a large bowl, combine the cucumber, onion, and bell pepper.

In a small bowl, whisk together the vinegar, oil, lavender, garlic, salt, and black pepper.

Drizzle the dressing on the cucumber mixture and let stand for at least 10 minutes.

Makes 4 servings

Per serving: 108 calories, 2 g protein, 11 g carbohydrates, 7 g fat, 0 mg cholesterol, 2 g fiber, 148 mg sodium

This lovely salad would be wonderful on a bed of heirloom oak leaf lettuce with a bit of the vinaigrette drizzled over all. I like to use lemon cucumbers, but any cucumbers will be delicious.

KITCHEN TIPS

If you like, peel the cucumbers, and if you want a less watery salad, seed the cucumbers by running the tip of a teaspoon down the center.

A few years ago, my dear friend Michael Romano, chef at Union Square Café in New York City, took me to his home in the Hamptons. Rather than going out to eat as we always do when in the city, he cooked for me. We drank good wine and laughed and cried as friends do sometimes. But the most memorable part of the actual meal was his cipollini onions. This is my interpretation of his recipe.

KITCHEN TIP

Cipollini onions are ideal to cook alongside roasting meats or chicken. Add them at the very beginning; they impart flavor and act as a side dish.

BRAISED CIPOLLINI ONIONS

½–1	cup vegetable or chicken broth	2	tablespoons brown sugar
½	cup ruby port	2	tablespoons unsalted butter
1	tablespoon chopped fresh thyme	½	teaspoon salt
½	pound cipollini onions or other small onions		

Place ½ cup of the broth, the port, and thyme in a large skillet over high heat. Add the onions and bring to a boil. Reduce the heat to low, cover, and simmer for 30 minutes, or until the onions are very soft. Add the remaining ½ cup broth if all of the liquid evaporates.

When the onions are cooked, you should have ¼ cup reduced sauce. If you have more sauce, uncover and simmer over medium-high heat until reduced to ¼ cup.

Add the brown sugar, butter, and salt and cook, uncovered, stirring occasionally, for 5 minutes.

Makes 4 servings

Per serving: 147 calories, 1 g protein, 15 g carbohydrates, 6 g fat, 16 mg cholesterol, 2 g fiber, 368 mg sodium

MY FAVORITE TUNA SALAD

1 lemon, halved

2 tablespoons chopped fresh dill or 2 teaspoons dried

1 tuna steak (about 6 ounces)

3 tablespoons extra virgin olive oil

1 small onion, minced

2 celery ribs or 1 small fennel bulb, chopped

1½ tablespoons capers

2 teaspoons Dijon mustard

2 tablespoons chopped fresh parsley

2 teaspoons sugar

3 hard-cooked eggs, peeled and chopped

Salt

Freshly ground black pepper

1½ pounds mesclun or spring salad mix

1 avocado, pitted, peeled, and sliced

This fresh tuna salad is far superior to the canned version. Use it in sandwiches or serve it mounded on top of lettuce with an drizzle of olive oil, red wine vinegar, and salt and pepper.

Squeeze the juice from half of the lemon into a medium bowl. Slice the other lemon half and place in a small skillet with 1 cup water and the dill. Bring to a boil over high heat. Add the tuna, reduce the heat to low, and simmer for 6 minutes, or until the tuna is opaque. Drain and chill thoroughly.

Meanwhile, in the bowl with the lemon juice, whisk together the oil, onion, celery or fennel, capers, mustard, parsley, and sugar. Set aside.

When the tuna is chilled, break it into bite-size pieces. Add the tuna and eggs to the bowl with the lemon juice mixture. Season with salt and pepper to taste. Toss gently to coat.

Evenly divide the mesclun among 4 plates. Top with one-quarter of the tuna salad. Fan one-quarter of the avocado to the side of the tuna salad.

Makes 4 servings

Per serving: 326 calories, 20 g protein, 12 g carbohydrates, 24 g fat, 175 mg cholesterol, 8 g fiber, 252 mg sodium

KITCHEN TIPS

I love old-fashioned tuna melts. Mound lots of the tuna salad on a slice of bread, cover with a few slices of Jarlsberg or Cheddar cheese, and warm under the broiler.

When tomatoes are in season, add a few slices to tuna salads or sandwiches.

Fava beans, also known as faba or broad beans, are very common in the Mediterranean.

FAVA BEAN AND ORZO SALAD

4	ounces orzo or other small pasta	3	tablespoons chopped oil-packed sun-dried tomatoes
2	pounds whole fava beans	3	tablespoons red wine vinegar
3	tablespoons extra virgin olive oil		Juice of 1 lemon
1	red onion, thinly sliced	½	teaspoon salt
2	garlic cloves, minced	½	teaspoon freshly ground black pepper
1½	tablespoons chopped fresh marjoram	1	bunch arugula (about 5 ounces)

KITCHEN TIP

You can substitute 3 cups fresh or frozen peas or lima beans for the fava beans.

Cook the orzo according to package directions; drain.

Meanwhile, bring a large pot of water to a boil over high heat. Working in batches if necessary, boil the beans for 6 minutes, or until the inner beans are tender but not mushy. Cool slightly. Remove and discard the outer pods. Using a small sharp knife, remove the outer skin of the beans.

Heat the oil in a large skillet over medium heat. Add the onion and garlic and cook for 7 minutes, or until very soft. Remove from the heat and stir in the marjoram, tomatoes, vinegar, lemon juice, salt, and pepper. Add the beans and orzo and toss to coat well.

Divide the arugula among 4 salad plates. Top with the bean salad.

Makes 4 servings
Per serving: 368 calories, 15 g protein, 54 g carbohydrates, 12 g fat, 0 mg cholesterol, 10 g fiber, 360 mg sodium

This refreshing and light dessert is welcomed by most, even after a big meal. It can be made with either fresh or frozen berries. When in season, in addition to the berries, float bite-size pieces of melon in the soup. This soup is delicious served with crème fraîche or vanilla yogurt.

KITCHEN TIP

Consider serving the soup as a warm dessert with ginger cookies.

SUMMER FRUIT SOUP

1	quart very ripe strawberries, hulled	2	tablespoons balsamic vinegar
1	cup dry white wine	1	cinnamon stick
3	cups orange juice	2	whole star anise
½	cup honey	3	whole black peppercorns
	Zest of 1 lime	1	teaspoon salt
	Juice of 2 limes	3	cups berries (such as raspberries, blueberries, or blackberries)
2	tablespoons chopped fresh mint		

In a large saucepan, combine the strawberries, wine, orange juice, honey, lime zest, lime juice, mint, vinegar, cinnamon stick, star anise, peppercorns, and salt. Bring to a simmer over medium heat and cook for 15 minutes for the flavors to blend. Remove from the heat and cool to room temperature. Remove and discard the cinnamon stick and star anise.

Place a food mill over a large bowl. Pour the soup through the mill and press into the bowl. Discard the seeds.

Chill the fruit broth. When ready to serve, ladle the broth into shallow bowls. Sprinkle generously with berries.

Makes 6 servings

Per serving: 255 calories, 3 g protein, 56 g carbohydrates, 1 g fat, 4 mg cholesterol, 7 g fiber, 205 mg sodium

BASIL-LEMON CAKE

2½ cups cake flour

2½ teaspoons baking powder

½ teaspoon salt

½ cup butter, softened

1½ cups granulated sugar

2 large eggs, beaten

½ cup chopped fresh basil

2 tablespoons finely grated lemon zest

1 teaspoon vanilla extract

1 cup + 2 tablespoons buttermilk

1½ cups mixed berries (such as raspberries or blackberries)

Preheat the oven to 375°F. Lightly oil a 9" springform pan.

In a medium bowl, combine the flour, baking powder, and salt.

Place the butter and granulated sugar in a large bowl. With an electric mixer on medium speed, beat until creamy. Add the eggs, basil, lemon zest, and vanilla extract. Beat until blended.

Add the flour mixture, a third at a time, alternating with the buttermilk and beating on low speed until smooth.

Pour into the prepared pan. Bake for 35 to 45 minutes, or until a wooden pick inserted in the center comes out clean. Cool on a rack for 10 minutes. Remove the sides of the pan and cool completely.

Place on a serving plate and top with the berries.

Makes 12 servings

Per serving: 278 calories, 4 g protein, 45 g carbohydrates, 9 g fat, 58 mg cholesterol, 2 g fiber, 298 mg sodium

Although a basil cake sounds unusual, think of the basil as you would mint rather than as an herb used only in savory cooking. Mash cherries, berries, or any juicy sweet fruit and serve them over the cake with chocolate ice cream or whipped cream for an unbelievably luscious dessert.

(photograph on page 107)

KITCHEN TIP

This cake actually gets better the next day. Cover it well, but do not refrigerate it unless you need to store it for more than a day or two.

CREAM CHEESE–GLAZED SPONGE CAKE

Cake

1	cup fruit juice (such as peach-mango, strawberry-guava, or orange)	1	teaspoon baking powder
6	eggs, separated	1	teaspoon cinnamon
¾	teaspoon cream of tartar	½	teaspoon salt
1½	cups sugar	3	tablespoons citrus zest (such as orange, lemon, or lime)
1½	cups sifted whole grain pastry flour		

Glaze

½	cup sugar	1	teaspoon vanilla extract
3	tablespoons boiling water	½	cup finely chopped walnuts
8	ounces cream cheese, softened		Orange zest

To make the cake: Preheat the oven to 350°F.

In a small saucepan over medium-high heat, cook the fruit juice for 10 minutes, or until reduced to ½ cup. Cool to room temperature.

Place the egg whites in a large bowl. With an electric mixer on high speed, beat the egg whites and cream of tartar until soft peaks form. Gradually add ½ cup of the sugar, beating until stiff peaks form.

Place the egg yolks in another large bowl. Using the same beaters, on low speed, beat the egg yolks until light and fluffy. Gradually add the remaining 1 cup sugar and beat until creamy. Beat in the flour, baking powder, cinnamon, salt, fruit juice, and citrus zest just until blended. Pour the yolk mixture over the egg whites and gently fold in until combined.

Pour into an ungreased 10" tube pan. Bake for 45 minutes, or until a wooden pick inserted in the center comes out clean. Invert onto a heavy long-necked bottle to cool completely.

To make the glaze: Meanwhile, place the sugar in a large heat-safe bowl. Add the water and stir for 2 minutes, or until the sugar melts. Cool slightly.

Add the cream cheese and vanilla extract. Beat with an electric mixer on medium speed until smooth and well-blended.

When the cake is cool, invert onto a plate. Spread the glaze over the top of the cake. Sprinkle with the walnuts and orange zest.

Makes 16 servings

Per serving: 272 calories, 6 g protein, 38 g carbohydrates, 11 g fat, 95 mg cholesterol, 1 g fiber, 164 mg sodium

Basil-Lemon Cake (page 105) and Cream Cheese–Glazed Sponge Cake

FRESH BERRY PIE

Crust

½	cup whole grain pastry flour	1	teaspoon sugar
½	cup whole wheat flour	¼	teaspoon salt
1	teaspoon ground cinnamon	½	cup unsalted butter
		⅓	cup ice water

Filling

6	cups fresh berries (blackberries, raspberries, or blueberries) or 18 ounces partially thawed frozen berries	1¼	cups sugar
		3	tablespoons tapioca
			Zest of 1 lemon
		1	tablespoon lemon juice

Preheat the oven to 350°F.

To make the crust: In a large bowl, combine the pastry flour, whole wheat flour, cinnamon, sugar, and salt. Grate the butter into the flour mixture. Using your hands or a pastry blender, work the butter into the flour mixture until the pieces are about the size of peas.

Add the water, 1 tablespoon at a time, and blend until a soft, moist dough forms. Form the dough into a flat round disk. Wrap in plastic wrap and refrigerate for at least 1 hour.

To make the filling: When the dough is chilled, in a medium bowl, combine the berries, sugar, tapioca, lemon zest, and lemon juice. Toss to coat well.

Place the dough on a well-floured surface and roll to about ⅛" thickness, turning the dough often to keep it well-floured. Fold the dough in half and place in a 9" or 10" pie plate. Turn under and crimp the crust. Spoon the berry filling into the crust.

Bake for 1 hour, or until the crust is lightly browned. Place on a rack to cool for at least 30 minutes before slicing.

Makes 10 servings

Per serving: 272 calories, 2 g protein, 45 g carbohydrates, 10 g fat, 26 mg cholesterol, 6 g fiber, 60 mg sodium

Use a variety of berries in this pie. My favorites are blackberries, raspberries, and blueberries. Strawberries are too juicy for this pie, so save them for another recipe. I like to make my pies in a 10" glass pie plate. It allows me to see the crust baking, and I love to hear people ooh and ah over a big old beautiful pie.

KITCHEN TIP

Most people like ice cream or whipped cream with their pie, but because of the sweetness of the filling in this pie, I prefer a big dollop of sour cream.

MID-SUMMER

$\mathbf{A}$h, summertime, and the cookin' is easy. I find myself motivated to make salads and dishes that don't require a lot of stove time. The outdoor grill gets more attention as I enjoy roasting and grilling fresh vegetables for pastas, salads, and appetizers.

Everywhere, gardens are growing in full stride. This is the opposite of deep winter: So many varieties of fruits and vegetables are in abundance. I celebrate this bounty. I also remind myself not to let the sheer volume stop me from appreciating and enjoying the pleasure that each fruit and vegetable offers.

A visit to a farmers' market in midsummer can make me feel like a kid in a candy shop. The selection in summer is almost too enticing, even to me at times. All too often, as I unpack my overflowing basket at home, I wonder what I was thinking and how I will have the time to prepare this bounty. Then I motivate myself to prepare as much as possible for easy use during the week ahead.

For example, I pull out my trusty steamer and steam as many fresh items from my basket as possible. I remind myself that this hour or two that I spend on a weekend will reward me with timesaving meals during the week. My refrigerator is stocked with organic vegetables, fruits, salads, and even steamed fish. They can be eaten as is or with a little seasoning, added to pastas, grains, meats, and poultry, used as side dishes, or tossed in a vinaigrette.

As much as I love to indulge in luscious kinds of foods, my regular day-to-day diet consists of lots of vegetables and protein. This is amongst a handful of dishes that I could easily eat once or twice a week for lunch because it is a flavorful way of getting both.

BLOODY MARY SHRIMP COCKTAIL

4	cups tomato juice	½	teaspoon salt
2	limes	¼–½	teaspoon hot-pepper sauce
1	teaspoon Worcestershire sauce		
2	tablespoons sugar	1	small cucumber, peeled, halved, and chopped
1	heaping tablespoon grated horseradish	1	avocado, pitted, peeled, and chopped
2	tablespoons grated red onion	2	green onions, sliced
½	teaspoon freshly ground black pepper	1	pound cooked shrimp, peeled and deveined

In a pitcher or large bowl, combine the tomato juice, juice from 1½ of the limes, the Worcestershire sauce, sugar, horseradish, red onion, and black pepper. Mix thoroughly and add the salt. Add the hot-pepper sauce to taste. Refrigerate.

In a medium bowl, combine the cucumber, avocado, and green onions. Toss with the juice of the remaining lime half.

Divide the shrimp among 4 parfait or milkshake glasses. Pour the tomato juice mixture on top. Top with the cucumber mixture. Serve chilled.

Makes 4 servings

Per serving: 182 calories, 18 g protein, 17 g carbohydrates, 6 g fat, 147 mg cholesterol, 3 g fiber, 781 mg sodium

MELON WRAPPED IN SMOKED TURKEY

This is an adaptation of the classic prosciutto and melon dish. It is splendid with this fresh strawberry sauce.

6	very ripe strawberries, hulled		1	small summer melon (such as cantaloupe or honeydew)
¾	cup plain yogurt or sour cream		8–10	ounces thinly sliced smoked or oven-roasted turkey breast (about 16 slices)
1	tablespoon honey		8	fresh chives, snipped
2	tablespoons chopped fresh mint			Sprinkle of ground red pepper (optional)
1	tablespoon chopped fresh chives			

Place the strawberries in a blender. Process until pureed. Place in a small serving bowl. Add the yogurt or sour cream, honey, mint, and chopped chives. Stir to blend well.

Cut the melon in half and scoop out the seeds. Place the melon, cut side down, on a cutting board. Using a sharp knife, remove and discard the rind. Cut into ¾"-thick wedges.

Wrap each melon wedge with a slice of the turkey. Top with the snipped chives and sprinkle with the pepper, if using. Serve with the strawberry sauce.

Makes 4 servings

Per serving: 198 calories, 24 g protein, 20 g carbohydrates, 3 g fat, 65 mg cholesterol, 1 g fiber, 73 mg sodium

KITCHEN TIPS

If you want to add spice to the dish, add a fresh chile pepper or two when you roast the bell peppers.

To make this dish more substantial for a great lunch entrée, place slices of meat or chicken on top of the peppers.

GARLIC BREAD WITH ROASTED SWEET PEPPERS

1	pound red or yellow bell peppers	¼	teaspoon freshly ground black pepper
2	tablespoons balsamic vinegar	4	tablespoons butter, softened
1	tablespoon extra virgin olive oil	3	garlic cloves, minced
2	tablespoons chopped fresh chives	¾	teaspoon paprika
2	tablespoons chopped fresh sage or basil	1	medium loaf Italian bread
¼	teaspoon salt	1	cup (4 ounces) grated Parmesan or hard Italian cheese

Preheat the oven to 400°F.

Place the peppers on a baking sheet. Bake for 15 minutes. When they are slightly blackened and the skin is blistering on one side, turn them and cook for 15 minutes longer. Remove from the oven but do not turn off the oven. Place the peppers in a large bowl. Cover with a plate or plastic wrap. Let cool for 15 minutes.

Peel off and discard the skins and remove and discard the seeds and stem. Slice or tear the peppers into narrow strips. Place in the bowl. Add the vinegar, oil, chives, sage or basil, salt, and pepper. Toss to coat well. Set aside.

In a small bowl, combine the butter, garlic, and paprika. Slice the bread horizontally in half lengthwise. If the bread is thick, remove some of the inside, leaving a hollow shell. Place the bread, cut side up, on a baking sheet. Spread thinly with the garlic butter. Sprinkle with the cheese. Bake for 15 minutes, or until lightly browned.

Place the bottom bread half on a cutting board. Arrange the roasted peppers on the bread half. Top with the other bread half. Press lightly. Cut crosswise into 10 slices.

Makes 10 servings

Per servings: 222 calories, 8 g protein, 24 g carbohydrates, 11 g fat, 21 mg cholesterol, 2 g fiber, 448 mg sodium

GREEK SALAD SANDWICHES

2 cups fresh shelling beans (such as fava, lima, or cranberry), shelled

1 garlic clove, minced

1 tablespoon chopped fresh oregano

3 tablespoons extra virgin olive oil

6 ounces feta cheese, crumbled

Salt

Freshly ground black pepper

1 cucumber, peeled, halved, and thinly sliced

½ small red onion, thinly sliced

1 large tomato, seeded and chopped

2 tablespoons chopped fresh mint

2 tablespoons chopped fresh parsley

Juice of 1 lemon

6 large whole wheat pitas (8" diameter)

Preheat the oven to 375°F.

Bring 1 cup water to a boil in a small saucepan over medium heat. Add the beans. Simmer for 10 to 15 minutes, or until soft. Using a small knife, remove the outer skin of the beans. Place the beans and the cooking liquid in a medium bowl. Mash with a potato masher or fork. Add the garlic, oregano, and 1½ tablespoons of the oil. Stir in the cheese. Season with salt and pepper to taste. Set aside.

In a medium serving bowl, combine the cucumbers, onion, tomato, mint, parsley, lemon juice, and the remaining 1½ tablespoons oil. Season with salt and pepper to taste.

Cut the pitas in half and open to form pockets. Evenly divide and spread the bean mixture into the pitas. Gently press together. Place on a baking sheet and cover with foil. Bake for 10 minutes, or until warmed. Remove from the oven and cut into halves or quarters.

Place the cucumber salad in the middle of a large platter. Surround with the bean sandwiches.

Makes 6 servings

Per serving: 325 calories, 14 g protein, 39 g carbohydrates, 14 g fat, 25 mg cholesterol, 10 g fiber, 489 mg sodium

There is little that compares with just-harvested shelling beans. Mashed with a little feta cheese and olive oil and warmed inside a pita, to me, it's heavenly. Next to the simple tomato-cucumber salad, not only is this a healthy meal but it is full of a wonderful range of Mediterranean flavors.

KITCHEN TIP

If you don't grow or can't find shelling beans at your market, there are excellent canned whole organic beans. Simply mash rinsed and drained beans with a bit of the canning liquid until the consistency of hummus.

BRANDO'S GRILLED STEAK AND VEGETABLES

¼	cup olive oil		1	teaspoon salt
½	cup hearty red wine (such as zinfandel or Cabernet)		1	teaspoon freshly ground black pepper
2	tablespoons Worcestershire sauce		1	top sirloin or round steak (2 to 3 pounds)
¼	cup soy sauce		2	large onions, sliced thick
4	garlic cloves, minced		4	red and/or green bell peppers, sliced thick
2	large shallots, minced		1	medium eggplant, sliced thick
2	tablespoons Dijon mustard			
¼	cup brown sugar			

In a large measuring cup, combine the oil, wine, soy sauce, Worcestershire sauce, mustard, garlic, shallots, brown sugar, salt, and black pepper.

Place the steak in a resealable plastic bag and add half of the marinade. Place the onions, bell peppers, and eggplant in another resealable plastic bag and add the remaining half of the marinade. Seal both bags and place in the refrigerator for at least 1 hour or overnight.

Lightly oil a grill rack or broiler pan. Preheat the grill or broiler.

Remove the steak from the marinade, reserving the marinade. Place the steak on the rack or pan. Cook for 15 minutes, turning once, or until a thermometer inserted in the center registers 145°F for medium-rare. Let stand for 10 minutes before slicing.

Add the vegetables to the rack or pan during the last 7 minutes of cooking. Cook, turning occasionally, for 7 minutes, or until lightly browned.

Makes 8 servings

Per serving: 405 calories, 25 g protein, 22 g carbohydrates, 23 g fat, 76 mg cholesterol, 3 g fiber, 943 mg sodium

One Sunday afternoon, my friend Brando cooked dinner for me. I sat in front of the TV, typing away on my computer, sipping a glass of wine, banished from the kitchen and all cooking. For me, there is nothing as delicious as a simple meal of barbecued steak, mushrooms, peppers, and onions. And just having someone cook for me is a gift beyond compare.

KITCHEN TIPS

Marinate the ingredients overnight for deeper flavor and as a way to tenderize the meat.

This marinade is also a delicious salad dressing, especially over bitter greens and hearty lettuces.

KITCHEN TIP

Instead of sandwiches, give the kids these roulades for lunch. Cut into rounds, they make great finger food.

CHICKEN ROULADES WITH ROASTED PEPPER STUFFING

4	boneless, skinless chicken breast halves	4	ounces feta cheese, crumbled
3	bacon strips		Salt
1	tablespoon olive oil		Freshly ground black pepper
½	red onion, finely chopped		
1	large red bell pepper, thinly sliced	3	tablespoons Dijon mustard
		1	tablespoon honey
3	tablespoons chopped fresh basil	½	teaspoon ground cumin

Preheat the oven to 375°F. Lightly oil an 8" baking pan.

If you can, get your butcher to pound the chicken breasts. Otherwise, pound the chicken breasts to about ¼" thickness.

In a large skillet over medium-high heat, cook the bacon until crisp. Place on a paper towel. Discard the bacon fat.

Add the oil to the skillet. Add the onion and bell pepper. Cover and cook, stirring occasionally, over medium heat for 10 to 15 minutes, or until the vegetables are very soft. Remove from the heat. Add the basil and cool to room temperature. Stir in the cheese.

Season the chicken with salt and black pepper to taste. Evenly divide the onion mixture among the chicken breast halves. Roll them jelly-roll style to form the roulades. Place in the prepared baking dish.

In a small bowl, combine the mustard, honey, and cumin. Evenly divide among the roulades, spreading to coat.

Bake for 30 minutes, or until the chicken is opaque and the juices run clear.

Makes 4 servings

Per serving: 261 calories, 26 g protein, 10 g carbohydrates, 13 g fat, 76 mg cholesterol, 1 g fiber, 473 mg sodium

Chicken Roulades with Roasted Pepper Stuffing and Fresh Corn and Bean Succotash (page 133)

Odessa Piper

L'Etoile, Madison, Wisconsin

We at L'Etoile believe that respect for nature and all that grows is the beginning of the understanding of good food. We strive to work with ingredients that are cultivated in accordance with their natural cycles and in their native and adapted soils. The artisanal skills that evolve through this understanding are the heartbeat of great cultures and will guide the development of our own.

L'ETOILE SUCCOTASH

1 cup purple pearl onions	½ pound green beans, cut into ½" pieces
4 cloves garlic	1 medium yellow onion, diced
3 tablespoons olive oil	3 green onions, chopped
4 tablespoons balsamic vinegar	1 cup cherry tomatoes, quartered
4 tablespoons rice vinegar	¼ cup small fresh basil leaves
8 ears corn, shucked	1 tablespoon fresh tarragon leaves
1 red bell pepper	1 tablespoon fresh dill leaves
1 green bell pepper	Salt and freshly ground black pepper
½ pound fingerling potatoes	

Heat the oven to 375°. Place the pearl onions and garlic cloves in a roasting pan. Toss with 1 tablespoon of the oil and the balsamic vinegar. Cover and roast for 30 minutes. Set the onions aside. Remove the garlic to a small bowl with any juices and mash into a paste. Stir in the rice vinegar. Set aside.

Heat a grill to medium-high. Place the corn and bell peppers on the grill and cook, turning often, until completely charred. Set the corn aside to cool. Place the peppers in a covered bowl for 10 minutes, or until cool enough to handle. Slip off the skins and remove the stems and seeds. Slice the peppers into bite-size strips. Set aside. Remove the corn from the cobs by standing them upright and cutting off the kernels with vertical slices. Slice the blade down the cob for a second pass to include the tender germ. Set aside.

Place the potatoes in a medium saucepan and cover with salted water. Bring to a boil over high heat. Reduce the heat to low, cover, and simmer for 10 minutes, or until almost tender. Add the green beans and cook for 3 minutes longer, or until the potatoes are just tender and the green beans are tender-crisp. Drain and set aside.

In a large skillet, heat 2 tablespoons olive oil over medium-high heat. Cook the diced onion until transparent. Quickly add the potatoes and beans, roasted onions, peppers, and green onions in that order. When warm, add the roasted corn, stirring to warm through. Place in a large serving bowl and toss with the garlic-vinegar mixture, cherry tomatoes, and herbs. Season to taste with the salt and pepper.

Makes 8 servings

DEEP-DISH SUMMER VEGETABLE COBBLER

Crust

1½	cups unbleached all-purpose flour
¼	cup whole wheat flour or cornmeal
2½	teaspoons baking powder
½	teaspoon salt
¼	teaspoon ground red pepper (optional)

½	cup finely chopped fresh parsley
¼	cup cold butter, grated
1	cup (4 ounces) shredded Cheddar cheese
1	cup buttermilk

Filling

¼	cup butter
1	large shallot, minced
3	tablespoons unbleached all-purpose flour
2	cups milk or vegetable broth
¼	cup Madeira wine (optional)
2	tablespoons chopped fresh sage

3	cups cooked vegetables (such as zucchini, eggplant, fennel, and bell peppers), cut into bite-size pieces
½	teaspoon salt
¼	teaspoon freshly ground black pepper
1	cup (4 ounces) shredded Cheddar cheese

To make the crust: In a large bowl, combine the all-purpose flour, whole wheat flour or cornmeal, baking powder, salt, pepper (if using), and parsley. Cut in the butter. Add the cheese and stir in the buttermilk just until blended. Refrigerate while you make the filling.

To make the filling: Preheat the oven to 375°F. Lightly oil a 3-quart baking dish.

Melt the butter in a medium saucepan over medium heat. Add the shallot. Whisk in the flour. Cook, stirring constantly, for 3 minutes, or until the mixture turns golden brown. Slowly whisk in the milk or broth and wine, if using. Whisk until slightly thickened. Add the sage, vegetables, salt, and pepper.

Place the creamed vegetables in the prepared baking dish. Sprinkle with the cheese. Drop the crust batter by tablespoons on top of the vegetables. Bake for 20 minutes, or until the topping is browned. Remove from the oven and let stand for 10 minutes before serving.

Makes 6 servings

Per serving: 539 calories, 20 g protein, 43 g carbohydrates, 19 g fat, 91 mg cholesterol, 2 g fiber, 858 mg sodium

There are so many choices of vegetables to cook with at this time of the year. Use what you like, but make sure each is cooked to its own tenderness before adding to the sauce.

VEGETABLE STEW WITH POLENTA

Polenta

4	cups water	1	tablespoon chopped fresh rosemary
1	cup polenta		
½	cup (2 ounces) grated Asiago or Parmesan cheese		

Stew

2	tablespoons olive oil	3	cups vegetable or chicken broth
2	garlic cloves, minced		
1	onion, chopped	5	whole peppercorns
8	ounces shiitake mushrooms, stemmed and sliced	1	bay leaf
		8	large fresh herb sprigs (such as dill, oregano, basil, marjoram, sage)
1	large tomato, peeled, seeded, and chopped coarsely	3	tablespoons light miso or soy sauce
1	large carrot, sliced	⅔	cup fresh or frozen peas
1	small fennel bulb or 2 celery ribs, sliced	1	cup fresh or frozen corn kernels
2	potatoes, cubed		Chopped fresh parsley

To make the polenta: Lightly oil a 9" × 9" baking dish.

Bring the water to a boil in a medium saucepan over medium heat. Gradually add the polenta, whisking constantly. Cook, whisking often, for 30 minutes, or until the polenta thickens and is creamy. Stir in the cheese and rosemary.

Pour the polenta into the prepared baking dish. Smooth the top. Refrigerate for 30 minutes, or until firm.

To make the stew: Meanwhile, heat the oil in a large stockpot over medium heat. Add the garlic, onion, mushrooms, tomato, carrot, fennel or celery, and potatoes and cook, stirring occasionally, for 10 minutes. Add the broth, peppercorns, bay leaf, and herb sprigs.

In a small bowl, blend the miso or soy sauce with 2 tablespoons water until smooth. Add to the stockpot.

Bring to a boil over medium-high heat. Reduce the heat to low and simmer for 1½ hours, or until the flavor is full. Stir in the peas and corn.

Just before serving the stew, remove the polenta from the refrigerator and cut into 1" squares. Remove and discard the bay leaf and herb sprigs. Place 4 to 5 polenta squares in the bottom of 6 soup bowls and ladle the stew over the top. Garnish with the parsley.

Makes 6 servings

Per serving: 292 calories, 13 g protein, 44 g carbohydrates, 10 g fat, 7 mg cholesterol, 7 g fiber, 863 mg sodium

SAVORY MUSSEL STEW

2 tablespoons extra virgin olive oil

2 large shallots, chopped

8 ounces andouille sausage, chopped into ¼" pieces

4 garlic cloves, chopped

½ cup dry white wine

4 large tomatoes, peeled, seeded, and chopped

1 cup firmly packed basil leaves, cut into thin slices

2 tablespoons chopped fresh marjoram or oregano

1 teaspoon paprika

½ teaspoon freshly ground black pepper

2 cups clam juice

3 pounds mussels, scrubbed and beards removed

2 ounces Romano cheese, grated

Warm the oil in a large saucepan over medium heat. Add the shallots and sausage. Cook for 3 minutes. Stir in the garlic and wine and cook for 1 minute longer. Add the tomatoes, basil, marjoram or oregano, paprika, and pepper. Cook, stirring, for 2 minutes.

Add the clam juice, raise the heat to high, and bring to a boil. Reduce the heat to low. Add the mussels. Cover and simmer for 8 minutes, or until the mussels open. Discard any unopened mussels. Taste and adjust the seasoning.

Serve with the cheese.

Makes 6 servings

Per serving: 309 calories, 25 g protein, 13 g carbohydrates, 16 g fat, 59 mg cholesterol, 2 g fiber, 1,233 mg sodium

For me, the beauty and integrity of this dish come through the ingredients. Though this is a summer dish, it can also be wonderful on a cold winter's night, substituting canned organic tomatoes for the fresh. Be sure to serve with a loaf of dense crusty bread to dip into this lovely broth.

KITCHEN TIP

For a more refined and elegant dish, after completing the recipe, remove the mussels and dislodge the meat, discarding the shells. Add ½ cup heavy cream to the stew and simmer for 3 minutes over high heat. Add the mussels back in and mix thoroughly. Taste and adjust the seasoning.

There is nothing as comforting and delicious as a bowl of creamy risotto. During the summer months, taking advantage of fresh vegetables makes this dish a seasonal delight.

VEGETABLE RISOTTO WITH GOAT CHEESE

4   cups chicken or vegetable broth

2   tablespoons olive oil

1   fennel bulb, thinly sliced

2   garlic cloves, minced

1   cup Arborio rice

2   tablespoons chopped fresh mint or basil

1   cup fresh or frozen and thawed peas

1   tomato, seeded and chopped

4   ounces soft goat cheese (such as chèvre)

Bring the broth to a boil in a large saucepan over medium heat. Reduce the heat to low, cover, and simmer.

Heat the oil in a deep heavy saucepan over medium heat. Add the fennel, garlic, and rice. Cook for 5 minutes, or until the rice is golden brown. Begin adding the simmering broth, ½ cup at a time, and cook, stirring constantly, for 20 minutes, or until the broth is absorbed and the risotto begins to get creamy.

Stir in the mint or basil, peas, tomato, and goat cheese. Cook for 2 minutes.

Makes 4 servings

Per serving: 402 calories, 18 g protein, 55 g carbohydrates, 13 g fat, 13 mg cholesterol, 3 g fiber, 785 mg sodium

ZESTY ZUCCHINI QUESADILLAS

- 2 tablespoons olive oil
- 1 zucchini, shredded
- ½ red or yellow bell pepper, finely chopped
- 1 small red onion, thinly sliced
- 2 garlic cloves, minced
- 1 teaspoon ground cumin
- ¼ cup chopped fresh cilantro
- ¼ teaspoon salt
- ¼ teaspoon freshly ground black pepper
- 1 large tomato, seeded and chopped
- Juice of 1 lime
- 1 teaspoon chili powder
- ¼ teaspoon hot-pepper sauce (optional)
- 4 whole wheat or white flour tortillas (8" diameter)
- 2 tablespoons toasted pine nuts
- 2 cups (8 ounces) Monterey Jack cheese, shredded

A favorite appetizer in my restaurant, these quesadillas are the perfect way to use abundant zucchini and tomatoes. Serve as a light lunch along with a tossed salad.

Heat the oil in a medium skillet over medium heat. Add the zucchini, bell pepper, onion, garlic, and cumin. Cook for 5 minutes, or until all the vegetables are soft. Stir in the cilantro, salt, and black pepper. Set aside.

In a small bowl, combine the tomato, lime juice, chili powder, and hot-pepper sauce, if using.

Spread one-fourth of the zucchini mixture evenly on one half of each tortilla. Sprinkle each with 1½ teaspoons pine nuts and one-fourth of the cheese. Fold the tortillas in half.

In a large skillet over medium-low heat, cook the quesadillas for 5 minutes, turning once, until the cheese is melted.

Cut the quesadillas into wedges and top with a generous amount of the tomato mixture.

Makes 4 servings

Per serving: 444 calories, 18 g protein, 28 g carbohydrates, 31 g fat, 60 mg cholesterol, 3 g fiber, 561 mg sodium

Warm chunks of salmon are delicious on a bed of zesty arugula. The raspberry vinaigrette adds a sweetness that mellows out this dish perfectly.

SALMON SALAD WITH RASPBERRY VINAIGRETTE

½	pint raspberries		¾	cup whole wheat flour
¼	cup extra virgin olive oil		2	tablespoons finely chopped fresh chives
3	tablespoons balsamic vinegar		1	salmon fillet (about ¾ pound), skinned and cut into 4 pieces
2	tablespoons brown sugar			
4	fresh tarragon sprigs, finely chopped		1	large bunch (6 ounces) arugula, torn into bite-size pieces
1	garlic clove, minced			
½	teaspoon salt		1	large yellow or red tomato, cut into wedges
½	teaspoon freshly ground black pepper			

In a small bowl, mash the raspberries with a fork. Place a sieve over a medium saucepan and push the raspberries through, discarding the seeds. Add 2 tablespoons of the oil, the vinegar, brown sugar, tarragon, garlic, ¼ teaspoon of the salt, and ¼ teaspoon of the pepper. Place over low heat and bring to a simmer.

Meanwhile, in a pie plate, combine the flour, chives, and the remaining ¼ teaspoon each of salt and pepper. Coat the salmon with the flour mixture.

Heat the remaining 2 tablespoons oil in a medium skillet over medium-high heat. Add the salmon and cook for 7 to 8 minutes, turning once, or until just opaque.

Place the arugula and tomato in a serving bowl and toss with the warm vinaigrette. Break the salmon fillets into large pieces over top of the arugula.

Makes 4 servings
Per serving: 436 calories, 21 g protein, 31 g carbohydrates, 26 g fat, 47 mg cholesterol, 6 g fiber, 47 mg sodium

The first way I ever ate green tomatoes was my Dad's way, straight off the barbecue, smoky and succulent. Dad had an organic garden, and his tomatoes were the prize. We ate green tomatoes at both the beginning and the end of the season. To this day, though I love the crusty fried version, my favorite is hot off the grill.

GRILLED GREEN TOMATOES

4	large green tomatoes, sliced into ½"-thick slices	1	tablespoon chopped fresh oregano
¼	cup extra virgin olive oil		Salt
2	garlic cloves, minced		Freshly ground black pepper

Lightly oil the grill rack. Preheat the grill.

Place the tomatoes in a large bowl. Add the oil, garlic, and oregano. Toss the tomatoes to thoroughly coat. Place the tomatoes on the grill and season each side generously with salt and pepper.

Cook, turning, for 5 minutes, or until the tomatoes are tender.

Makes 4 servings

Per serving: 96 calories, 2 g protein, 7 g carbohydrates, 7 g fat, 0 mg cholesterol, 1 g fiber, 16 mg sodium

KITCHEN TIPS

This is a perfect way to use those tomatoes that never quite ripened. When green tomatoes are picked when they are very firm, they will keep in the refrigerator in your vegetable bin for a few weeks.

While you have the grill hot, make extra tomatoes and re-frigerate for later use. They're great in scrambled eggs, on sandwiches, or as a side dish for grilled meats or poultry.

FRESH CORN AND BEAN SUCCOTASH

¼ pound green beans, cut into ½" pieces

2 ears corn, kernels removed

½ bell pepper, chopped

1 tomato, seeded and chopped

2 green onions, thinly sliced

1 jalapeño chile pepper, chopped

½ cup finely chopped fresh basil

½ teaspoon ground cumin

1 teaspoon sugar

Juice of 1 large lime

Salt

Freshly ground black pepper

Parsley

Fill a medium saucepan two-thirds full with water. Place over high heat and bring to a boil. Add the beans and corn. Cook for 3 minutes, or until tender-crisp. Drain and place in a large bowl.

Add the bell pepper, tomato, green onions, chile pepper, basil, cumin, sugar, and lime juice. Season with salt and black pepper to taste. Sprinkle with parsley. Toss to coat well.

Makes 4 servings

Per serving: 73 calories, 3 g protein, 16 g carbohydrates, 1 g fat, 0 mg cholesterol, 3 g fiber, 14 mg sodium

Just-picked corn and beans barely need to be cooked. Tossed together in this light dish, I can't seem to get enough. For a luscious touch, finish with a dollop of sour cream. This is a dish that should be eaten with a spoon, gathering all the flavors to savor each and every bite.

(photograph on page 119)

KITCHEN TIP

On a warm summer night, serve this dish as a complete meal with chilled seafood or a grilled lamb or pork chop.

Just-warmed tomatoes, lightly crisped on top with buttered bread crumbs . . . a loaf of warm olive or herb bread . . . served with a butter lettuce salad . . . This is my idea of a perfect light dinner on a hot summer's night.

KITCHEN TIP

For a heartier meal, serve the tomatoes on top of cooked pasta that has been tossed with olive oil, garlic, and plenty of fresh basil.

TOMATOES WITH GOAT CHEESE

4 medium beefsteak tomatoes, halved crosswise and seeded

Salt

Freshly ground black pepper

6 ounces soft goat cheese (such as chèvre), at room temperature

¾ cup dry bread crumbs

2 tablespoons chopped fresh thyme

¼ cup extra virgin olive oil

2 tablespoons balsamic vinegar

2 tablespoons chopped fresh chives

1 large garlic clove, minced

Preheat the oven to 350°F. Lightly oil a baking sheet.

Place the tomatoes, cut side up, on the prepared baking sheet. Season generously with salt and pepper.

In a small bowl, blend the cheese with the bread crumbs and thyme. Evenly divide the mixture over the top of the tomatoes, pushing some of the bread crumbs into the tomatoes. Bake for 20 minutes, or until warmed thoroughly.

Meanwhile, in another small bowl, whisk the oil, vinegar, chives, and garlic. Season with salt and pepper to taste.

Remove the tomatoes from the oven and let stand for 10 minutes. Place the tomatoes on a serving plate and drizzle with the dressing.

Makes 4 servings

Per serving: 401 calories, 14 g protein, 33 g carbohydrates, 24 g fat, 20 mg cholesterol, 4 g fiber, 409 mg sodium

MEXICAN CHOCOLATE PUDDING

2	cups whole milk	1	cinnamon stick, broken in half
5	ounces unsweetened chocolate, grated		
		6	egg yolks
¾	cup sugar	1	teaspoon vanilla extract

In a small saucepan over medium heat, warm the milk, chocolate, sugar, and cinnamon stick. Cook, stirring often, for 5 minutes, or until the chocolate melts. Set aside for 15 minutes.

Return the saucepan to medium heat and bring the mixture to a simmer, whisking occasionally. Remove from the heat. Remove and discard the cinnamon stick.

Place the egg yolks in a medium bowl and beat lightly. Gradually whisk in half of the milk mixture. Gradually whisk the egg mixture back into the milk mixture. Add the vanilla extract.

Return the saucepan to medium heat and cook for 3 minutes, or until simmering and the pudding coats the back of a spoon.

Pour into 6 custard cups. Cover each with plastic wrap and refrigerate for at least 2 hours.

Makes 6 servings

Per serving: 328 calories, 8 g protein, 35 g carbohydrates, 21 g fat, 224 mg cholesterol, 4 g fiber, 51 mg sodium

I like to serve this dish with gingersnaps and organic strawberries for a lovely presentation.

KITCHEN TIP

This custard is wonderful warm, and before refrigeration, it tends to be looser. It is lovely poured warm over berries or as a rich sauce on cakes.

KITCHEN TIP

Organic frozen fruit can also
be used. Thaw it first, and if
the fruit is juicy, cut down on
the amount of yogurt.

SUMMER FRUIT PIZZA

4	small prebaked pizza crusts (6" diameter)	⅓	cup cherries, halved and pitted
¾	cup (6 ounces) vanilla or strawberry yogurt	⅓	cup blueberries or raspberries
½	cup sugar	2	figs, quartered
1	teaspoon ground cinnamon	½	cup chopped fresh basil
2	small apricots, pitted and sliced	1	tablespoon lemon zest
1	medium peach, pitted and sliced	2	cups (8 ounces) shredded Cheddar cheese
		½	cup (2 ounces) grated Parmesan cheese

Preheat the oven to 450°F.

Place the crusts on a baking sheet. Spread the crusts generously with the yogurt.

Sprinkle ¼ cup of the sugar and ½ teaspoon of the cinnamon evenly over the yogurt.

Arrange the apricots, peach, cherries, blueberries or raspberries, and figs on the yogurt. Sprinkle with the basil, lemon zest, the remaining ¼ cup sugar, and the remaining ½ teaspoon cinnamon. Top with the cheeses.

Bake for 7 minutes, or until the cheese is browned and the pizza is warm throughout. Remove from the oven and let stand for 5 minutes before serving.

Makes 4 servings

Per serving: 494 calories, 22 g protein, 51 g carbohydrates, 24 g fat, 72 mg cholesterol, 4 g fiber, 611 mg sodium

WATERMELON-ROSEMARY ICE

1   cup sugar
1   cup water
3   cups watermelon puree

1   tablespoon fresh lemon juice
1   tablespoon finely chopped fresh rosemary

Place a 9" × 9" metal baking pan in the freezer.

In a small saucepan over medium-high heat, bring the sugar and water to a boil. Boil for 5 minutes. Place in a large bowl and cool completely.

When cooled, add the watermelon puree, lemon juice, and rosemary. Pour into the frozen baking pan, cover with foil, and return to the freezer. Freeze, stirring occasionally, for 3 hours, or until partially frozen.

Place the mixture in a food processor with the metal blade attached. Process until smooth but still frozen. Return the mixture to the baking pan, cover, and freeze for 3 hours longer, or until frozen.

Remove from the freezer 15 minutes before serving. Scoop into dessert bowls.

Makes 8 servings

Per serving: 138 calories, 1 g protein, 34 g carbohydrates, 0 g fat, 0 mg cholesterol, 0 g fiber, 3 mg sodium

Watermelon is the epitome of summer, and I love it made into this cool, refreshing dessert on a hot summer day. The rosemary and lemon highlight the watermelon in a most pleasing way.

KITCHEN TIP

Sorbets are smoothest when prepared in an ice cream maker. If you have one, pour the mixture into the container of your maker and prepare according to manufacturer's directions.

CASCADIAN FARM®

Like many starry-eyed students in the early 1970s, Gene Kahn dreamed of living off the land.

The difference is, he actually did.

In 1972, Kahn waved goodbye to the University of Washington's graduate school of English, packed his poetry books, and moved to Washington's Upper Skagit Valley. In the shadow of the majestic North Cascade Mountains, he leased a ramshackle farmhouse with a couple of acres of land and started growing organic carrots and sugar peas.

During the day, he worked like a peasant. At night, he pored through antique farming books that fueled his romantic vision.

"I regard Nature as the supreme farmer," he says. "Study Nature, and the answers become evident."

With the help of free-thinking friends, Cascadian Farm blossomed. Kahn soon had more than enough food to feed himself, so he sold his excess produce at farmers' markets in Seattle. Still, he realized that he would have to master the basics of processing, distribution, and marketing if the farm was going to reach its full potential.

Plowing the organic fields of Cascadian Farm

Courtesy of Cascadian Farm

He made a few mistakes and learned along the way. When he realized that organic strawberries have an extremely short shelf life, he turned lemons into lemonade, or, to be more precise, fresh strawberries into organic strawberry jam. Soon, his line of jams also included blackberry, peach, apricot, dark cherry, blueberry, raspberry, and Concord grape.

Today, Cascadian Farm is a major player in the natural foods market, with more than 150 organic products in seven categories: frozen desserts, frozen vegetables, vegetarian meals, frozen fruits, frozen juices, pickles and kraut, and, of course, jam.

Frozen fruits and vegetables are the heart of Cascadian Farm's products. With more than 35 products, the company is the leading organic producer on supermarket freezer shelves. Along with favorite frozen vegetables, such as peas, corn, and broccoli, Cascadian Farm now sells more exotic items such as edamame, and Szechuan green beans.

Cascadian Farm even produces organic frozen entrées. Their innovative and organic product line includes Three Cheese Pasta with Sweet Red Peppers, Spinach Lasagna, and Fiesta Vegetarian Enchiladas.

Although Kahn's ingredients now come from organic farmers throughout the Pacific Northwest, he hasn't abandoned the farm. His original homestead—the Cascadian Home Farm—is now a 20-acre oasis of fruits, vegetables, and herbs where tomorrow's organic farmers serve apprenticeships.

Although Kahn has made the transition from subsistence farmer to successful entrepreneur, he hasn't lost the idealism that inspired his 30-year organic odyssey.

"The native prairies of the United States were farmed for decades without the addition of synthetic pesticides or fertilizers," he says. "By integrating plants and animals, crops and livestock, we create a unique culture of mixed farming . . . an imitation of Nature's perfect system."

Courtesy of Cascadian Farm

Organic raspberry harvest at Cascadian Farm

INDIAN SUMMER

At summer's end, when the memory of vacation fades, the routines of school and work urge me back to my kitchen. The days of casual summer dining subside, and the meaningfulness of being surrounded by family and friends for a leisurely meal returns.

Indian summer is a time of large platters overloaded with the bounty of just-picked goodness. It is a time to celebrate the harvest with family and friends and speak of fond memories of summer. It is also a time to honor and cherish the last summer crops, such as tomatoes and raspberries. I also give open-arm welcomes to baby acorn squash, broccoli, kale, chard, and other early fall crop arrivals. All earn prominent places on my dining room table.

Aware of the juxtaposition of seasons that Indian summer represents, conserving for the cold months ahead becomes a priority for me both at

home and at my restaurant. My two food dryers are working nearly every night, the racks filled with tomatoes, peppers, eggplant, figs, and even berries. At the same time, herbs hang in bunches above my kitchen cabinets. Green tomatoes, cucumbers, beans, baby onions, and even Brussels sprouts are saved in jars filled with herbal or chile-infused vinegar.

Indian summer represents a season of preparation for the colder months to come. As the sweetness of summer disappears, I feel satisfied in knowing that I have created a kitchen ready for winter.

Recipes

I like to cook these figs on rosemary skewers, which lightly scents the figs during cooking. To make the skewers, choose straight branches. Run your hand down the branch against the grain of the needles and remove them. Place the unused rosemary in a jar to dry and use throughout the autumn season.

ROSEMARY GRILLED FIGS

½ cup hearty red wine (such as zinfandel or Cabernet)

½ pint raspberries

1 teaspoon chopped fresh rosemary

1 tablespoon brown sugar

2 tablespoons balsamic vinegar

8 brown or green figs

4 very thin slices lean prosciutto, halved

Place four 6" rosemary or wooden skewers in a shallow baking dish. Add the wine and soak for 30 minutes. Remove the skewers and set aside. Add the raspberries, rosemary, brown sugar, and vinegar to the wine and mash with a fork.

Lightly oil the grill rack or broiler pan. Preheat the grill or broiler to medium heat.

Meanwhile, wrap each fig with a half-piece of the prosciutto. Thread 2 figs onto each skewer.

Place the figs on the rack or pan. Grill or broil the figs, turning often, for 5 minutes, or until they are warmed thoroughly. Serve with the raspberry sauce.

Makes 4 servings

Per serving: 219 calories, 4 g protein, 35 g carbohydrates, 5 g fat, 12 mg cholesterol, 6 g fiber, 287 mg sodium

Rosemary Grilled Figs and Warm Brie with Kumquats (page 146)

KITCHEN TIP

This recipe also makes a delicious sauce for sweets such as ice cream or angel food cake. Simply omit the onion and red-pepper flakes and increase the brown sugar to ½ cup.

WARM BRIE WITH KUMQUATS

8	ounces Brie or Camembert cheese
½	pound kumquats
1	tablespoon butter
1	small onion, thinly sliced
¼	cup packed brown sugar
¼	cup fruity white wine (such as Gewürztraminer) or white grape juice
⅛	teaspoon dried red-pepper flakes
	Salt
1	loaf thinly sliced whole wheat Italian bread (about 24 slices)

Place the cheese on a large plate and allow to warm to room temperature.

Meanwhile, wash the kumquats, remove the stems, and slice them into ⅛"-thin rounds. Place in a large bowl.

In a medium skillet over low heat, melt the butter. Add the onion and cook for 5 minutes, or until soft. Add the kumquats, cover, and simmer for 10 minutes, or until the kumquats are completely soft. Add the brown sugar, wine or grape juice, and red-pepper flakes and simmer for 15 minutes longer, or until the sauce is slightly thickened. Season with salt to taste. Cool slightly, then pour the sauce over the cheese. Serve immediately with the bread.

Makes 8 servings
Per serving: 253 calories, 10 g protein, 31 g carbohydrates, 10 g fat, 32 mg cholesterol, 5 g fiber, 183 mg sodium

LOLLY FONT'S ROASTED PEPPER BRUSCHETTA

2	large red bell peppers		Salt
2	tablespoons extra virgin olive oil		Freshly ground black pepper
2	large garlic cloves, minced	1	loaf semolina or Italian bread
2	tablespoons chopped fresh basil	4	ounces fresh mozzarella cheese, sliced
1	tablespoon chopped fresh parsley	¼	cup (1 ounce) grated Asiago or Parmesan cheese
1	tablespoon chopped fresh oregano		

Preheat the broiler.

Place the bell peppers on a broiler pan and broil, turning often, until the skin is charred black all over and is loosened. Place the peppers in a large pot with a lid. Cover and cool slightly.

Using your hands, peel the peppers over the pot, discarding the skin and reserving the juices. Tear the peppers in half and remove and discard the stems and seeds. Tear the peppers into big strips and add to the juices.

Add the oil, garlic, basil, parsley, and oregano to the pot. Season with salt and black pepper to taste. Toss and allow to marinate for at least 30 minutes.

Meanwhile, cut the bread in half lengthwise and place, cut side up, on the same broiler pan. Drizzle some of the pepper juices on the cut sides of the bread. Broil for 3 minutes, or until lightly browned.

Remove from the oven and cover the bread with the peppers, mozzarella, and grated cheese. Reduce the oven temperature to 400°F. Bake the bread for 15 minutes, or until the cheese is slightly melted. Slice each loaf half into 8 pieces.

Makes 8 servings

Per serving: 240 calories, 10 g protein, 31 g carbohydrates, 9 g fat, 11 mg cholesterol, 2 g fiber, 281 mg sodium

Lolly Font is a yoga teacher and one of the best cooks I know. She shops regularly at farmers' markets, choosing only organic foods and creating simple, impressive dishes by cooking with the season's best. When peppers are at their prime, she often prepares these roasted peppers for bruschetta or as a pasta sauce.

KITCHEN TIP

This pepper mixture makes a delicious pasta sauce. Prepare as directed and stir into 8 ounces of cooked pasta such as penne, rotini, or shells. Be sure to top with a generous sprinkling of grated cheese or a dollop of soft goat cheese.

BALSAMIC GLAZED GAME HEN

12	shallots, peeled	¼	cup packed brown sugar or honey
2	crisp apples (such as Granny Smith, pippin, or Red Delicious), peeled, cored, and sliced into thick wedges	¼	cup balsamic vinegar
		2	tablespoons Dijon mustard
		4	Cornish or rock game hens
2	tablespoons chopped fresh rosemary or lavender		Salt
			Freshly ground black pepper
1–2	cups chicken broth	¼	cup chopped fresh parsley

Preheat the oven to 500°F.

In a large roasting pan, combine the shallots, apples, rosemary or lavender, 1 cup of the broth, brown sugar or honey, vinegar, and mustard.

Season the hens generously with salt and pepper and place them on top of the shallot mixture. Reduce the oven temperature to 375°F and bake for 45 to 55 minutes, or until a thermometer inserted in the thickest portion registers 170°F and the juices run clear. Transfer the hens to 4 individual dinner plates, cover, and keep warm.

Stir the ingredients in the pan and cover with foil. Return the pan to the oven and roast for 10 minutes longer, or until the shallots are very soft, adding more broth to create plenty of juice, if necessary.

Spoon a generous amount of sauce over the top of each hen. Sprinkle with parsley.

Makes 4 servings

Per serving: 825 calories, 60 g protein, 33 g carbohydrates, 49 g fat, 337 mg cholesterol, 4 g fiber, 598 mg sodium

Game hen is a favorite around my house because it seems to hold its moisture more than chicken. As this dish bakes, the shallots and apples caramelize and blend into a thick, flavorful sauce that is wonderful spooned over the crispy skin of the hen.

These juicy burgers are delicious served with vegetables alongside them, but they make great sandwiches as well. Rather than buns, I actually like them squished with some vegetables between 2 slices of thick Italian bread with a generous spread of both mustard and ketchup.

KITCHEN TIP

To make an outrageous turkey meat loaf, double the amount of ground turkey, grated onion, parsley, salt, and pepper. Add a cup of bread crumbs and 2 eggs to the mixture. Form into a loaf pan and cover the top generously with ketchup. Bake in a 350°F oven for 45 minutes, or until a thermometer inserted in the center registers 160°F and the meat is no longer pink. Serve topped with the vegetables.

TURKEY BURGERS WITH VEGETABLE MÉLANGE

Burgers

1	pound ground turkey breast	1	teaspoon salt
1	small red onion, grated	½	teaspoon freshly ground black pepper
2	tablespoons chopped fresh parsley		

Vegetables

2	tablespoons extra virgin olive oil	2	tablespoons balsamic vinegar
3	garlic cloves, minced	1	tomato, chopped
1	onion, cut into wedges	¼	cup chopped fresh basil
1	medium Japanese eggplant, cut into ½" slices		Salt
1	medium green bell pepper, sliced		Freshly ground black pepper

To make the burgers: In a large bowl, combine the turkey, onion, parsley, salt, and pepper. Cover and refrigerate until ready to use.

To make the vegetables: Heat the oil in a large nonstick skillet over medium heat. Add the garlic, onion, eggplant, and bell pepper and cook, stirring frequently, for 8 minutes, or until tender. Add the vinegar and cook for 3 minutes, stirring to loosen the browned bits from the bottom of the pan. Add the tomato and basil and season with salt and black pepper to taste. Remove to a serving plate and keep warm.

Form the turkey mixture into 4 burgers and cook in the same skillet for 10 minutes, turning once, or until no longer pink. Place on the serving plate with the vegetables.

Makes 4 servings
Per serving: 262 calories, 31 g protein, 18 g carbohydrates, 8 g fat, 70 mg cholesterol, 6 g fiber, 648 mg sodium

HARVEST POT ROAST

1	large onion, cut into thick slices	2	tablespoons Dijon mustard
2	carrots, cut into 1" pieces	2	tablespoons Worcestershire sauce
12	ounces mushrooms, quartered	1	chuck roast (2½–3 pounds), trimmed of all visible fat
4	garlic cloves, minced	¼	teaspoon salt
1	can (14½ ounces) diced tomatoes, drained	¼	teaspoon freshly ground black pepper
1	cup ketchup		

Place the onion, carrots, mushrooms, garlic, and tomatoes in a slow cooker. In a small bowl, combine the ketchup, mustard, and Worcestershire sauce. Top the vegetables with half of the ketchup mixture.

Place the roast over the vegetables and sprinkle with the salt and pepper. Spread the remaining ketchup mixture over the roast. Cover and cook on low for 8 to 9 hours, or until the meat is very tender.

Let the meat stand for 10 minutes before slicing.

Makes 8 servings

Per serving: 478 calories, 56 g protein, 15 g carbohydrates, 21 g fat, 147 mg cholesterol, 2 g fiber, 709 mg sodium

On days when I am feeling especially decadent, I serve this pot roast with Horseradish Cream (see tip). Be sure to save some of the pot roast to make sandwiches the next day. Slice the meat, smoosh some of the vegetables, and place it between 2 slices of bread with Horseradish Cream or a smear of mustard.

KITCHEN TIP

I love this recipe served with this simple Horseradish Cream. In a small bowl, combine 1 cup sour cream, 3 tablespoons prepared horseradish, and 2 tablespoons sugar.

PORK 'N' PUMPKIN NOODLES

2	tablespoons olive oil		½	cup raisins
¾	pound pork loin, cut into 1" cubes		1	cinnamon stick
			1	cup chicken broth
1	medium pumpkin or butternut squash, cubed (about 2 cups)		1½	teaspoons paprika
			1	tablespoon chopped fresh thyme or 1 teaspoon dried
2	large leeks, whites only, thinly sliced and thoroughly washed		8	ounces buckwheat noodles
2	garlic cloves, minced		1½	cups sour cream

Heat the oil in a large skillet over medium heat. Add the pork and cook, turning frequently, for 6 minutes, or until cooked through. Remove to a large plate and keep warm.

Add the pumpkin or squash and leeks to the skillet and cook, stirring often, for 5 minutes, or until lightly browned. Add the garlic, raisins, cinnamon stick, broth, paprika, and thyme. Reduce the heat to low and simmer for 15 minutes, or until the squash is tender. Add the pork and simmer over low heat for 15 minutes.

Meanwhile, cook the noodles according to package directions. Drain and place in a large serving bowl.

Stir the sour cream into the pork mixture. Remove and discard the cinnamon stick. Pour the pork mixture over the noodles.

Makes 6 servings

Per serving: 481 calories, 24 g protein, 49 g carbohydrates, 23 g fat, 67 mg cholesterol, 4 g fiber, 537 mg sodium

The toasty flavor of the buckwheat stands up beautifully to the rustic combination of the pork and pumpkin.

KITCHEN TIP

Tuna is delicious when cooked rare, and many restaurants now serve it this way. If you're cooking it rare, be sure to purchase the highest quality tuna available, which is sushi-grade tuna, also known as Grade A.

BASIL-CRUSTED TUNA

1 tablespoon olive oil

2 tablespoons soy sauce

2 tablespoons mirin cooking wine

½ cup finely chopped fresh basil

¼ teaspoon coarsely ground black pepper

4 sushi-grade (Grade A) tuna steaks (about 1½ pounds)

1 green onion, thinly sliced

1 tablespoon finely chopped fresh ginger

1 garlic clove, minced

1 small red bell pepper, thinly sliced

½ hot chile pepper (such as jalapeño or cayenne), thinly sliced

2 bananas, cut into ¼"-thick slices

Chopped fresh basil

Preheat the broiler.

In a shallow bowl, combine the oil, soy sauce, wine, ½ cup basil, and black pepper. Add the tuna and marinate in the refrigerator for 15 to 30 minutes. Remove the tuna, reserving the marinade. Place on a broiler pan. Broil the tuna for 6 minutes, turning once, until browned and cooked to desired doneness. (With sushi-grade tuna, I prefer it as rare as possible. If not using sushi-grade, cook until opaque). Remove the tuna to a serving plate and keep warm.

Meanwhile, pour the remaining marinade into a medium skillet and add the green onion, ginger, garlic, bell pepper, and chile pepper. Cook, stirring frequently, over medium-high heat for 5 minutes. Add the bananas, remove from the heat, and toss to thoroughly coat the bananas. Spoon over the tuna and garnish with basil.

Makes 4 servings

Per serving: 245 calories, 28 g protein, 23 g carbohydrates, 5 g fat, 51 mg cholesterol, 3 g fiber, 566 mg sodium

Canned, frozen, or dried, cooked lima beans are fine in this salad, but if you grow limas in your garden, harvesting them fresh and tossing them into this salad is sublime.

KITCHEN TIP

The bean salad can be made days in advance, and the fish can be poached the night before for a quick and easy meal that is ready within minutes after a long day at work.

CHILLED SALMON WITH LIMA BEAN SALAD

2   cups cooked lima beans

½   red onion, thinly sliced

1   celery rib, thinly sliced

3   tablespoons sherry wine vinegar

3   tablespoons sugar

3   tablespoons chopped fresh parsley

    Salt

    Freshly ground black pepper

1½ cups vegetable or fish broth

¼   cup dry white wine or vermouth

3   large fresh tarragon sprigs, leaves removed and chopped

3   whole juniper berries or pink peppercorns (optional)

4   salmon fillets (1 pound)

1   head red leaf lettuce, washed and dried

1   large lemon, cut into 8 wedges

In a medium bowl, combine the beans, onion, celery, vinegar, sugar, and parsley. Season with salt and pepper to taste. Allow to marinate in the refrigerator for at least 30 minutes, tossing occasionally.

Meanwhile, in a large skillet over medium heat, cook the broth, wine, tarragon, and juniper berries or peppercorns for 5 minutes. Remove from the heat. Place the salmon in the broth and season with salt and pepper. Reduce the heat to low, cover, and simmer for 5 minutes, or until the fish is opaque. Remove from the heat and, using a slotted flat spatula, remove the fish to a serving plate. Cover and refrigerate for at least 30 minutes. Discard the broth.

To serve, evenly divide the lettuce among 4 plates. Spoon the bean salad in the center of each plate, reserving some of the marinade. Place the chilled salmon on top of the bean salad, drizzling with the remaining marinade. Serve with the lemon wedges.

Makes 4 servings

Per serving: 324 calories, 31 g protein, 36 g carbohydrates, 5 g fat, 60 mg cholesterol, 7 g fiber, 481 mg sodium

LAST-OF-THE-SUMMER FETTUCCINE

1 pound fresh fettucine

¼ cup extra virgin olive oil

1 small red onion, thinly sliced

½ red bell pepper, thinly sliced

2 large garlic cloves, minced

1 jalapeño chile pepper, seeded and minced

¼ cup tequila (optional)

2 large tomatoes, seeded and chopped

2 tablespoons chopped fresh oregano

½ cup chopped fresh cilantro

4 ounces feta cheese, crumbled

1 avocado, peeled, pitted, and chopped

Salt

Freshly ground black pepper

It is always interesting to see what the staff of a restaurant chooses frequently as their nightly employee meal. This is definitely an all-time favorite of mine at Flea St. Café.

Cook the fettuccine according to package directions. Drain and place in a large bowl.

Meanwhile, heat the oil in a large skillet over medium-high heat. Add the onion and bell pepper and cook for 2 minutes. Add the garlic, chile pepper, and tequila, if using, and cook for 1 minute longer. Add the tomatoes, oregano, and cilantro and cook for 3 minutes, or until the tomatoes are soft.

Stir the cheese and avocado into the skillet. Stir and season with salt and black pepper to taste. Add the sauce to the pasta and mix thoroughly.

Makes 4 servings

Per serving: 500 calories, 12 g protein, 41 g carbohydrates, 29 g fat, 62 mg cholesterol, 4 g fiber, 333 mg sodium

Stuffed Portobello Burgers and Frisée with Spicy Maple Pecans (page 165)

STUFFED PORTOBELLO BURGERS

3 tablespoons extra virgin olive oil

2 tablespoons balsamic vinegar

2 garlic cloves, minced

2 tablespoons chopped fresh basil

¼ teaspoon salt

¼ teaspoon freshly ground black pepper

4 large portobello mushrooms

1 small onion, finely chopped

1 small red bell pepper, finely chopped

¼ cup red wine

¾ cup toasted bread crumbs or finely crumbled bread

1½ cups (6 ounces) Monterey Jack cheese, shredded

4 whole wheat buns

Lightly oil the grill rack. Preheat the grill.

In a large bowl, combine the oil, vinegar, garlic, basil, salt, and black pepper. Spoon 2 tablespoons of the marinade into a medium skillet; set both aside.

Remove the stems from the caps of the mushrooms. Chop the stems into fine pieces. Place in a small bowl with the onion and bell pepper.

Using a teaspoon, scrape out and discard the gills of the mushroom caps. Place the mushroom caps in the bowl of marinade, tossing them to coat all sides.

Place the skillet with the marinade over medium heat and warm the marinade. Add the onion mixture and cook for 3 minutes, or until soft. Add the wine and continue cooking for another 3 to 4 minutes. Remove the skillet from the heat, add the bread crumbs, and mix thoroughly.

Place the mushroom caps, stem side down, on the grill and cook for 3 minutes. Remove and place on a platter and generously fill with stuffing. Evenly distribute the cheese on top of each. Return the mushrooms to the grill, stuffed side up. Cover and grill for 8 to 10 minutes, or until warm throughout. Tuck inside the buns.

Makes 4 servings

Per serving: 490 calories, 17 g protein, 42 g carbohydrates, 28 g fat, 54 mg cholesterol, 5 g fiber, 792 mg sodium

This recipe was inspired by John Garcia, co-owner of JJ & F Market in my neighborhood. He claims that he has seduced beef-burger eaters into believing that the flavor of this mushroom burger is as good or better than a meaty one. Even his kids like them, especially when tucked inside slightly warmed whole wheat buns.

KITCHEN TIP

For a lovely brunch idea, serve the creamed spinach over toasted English muffins topped with poached eggs instead of hard-cooked eggs.

OLD-FASHIONED CREAMED SPINACH

1	pound fresh spinach or 2 packages (10 ounces each) frozen	1½	cups milk
4	strips thick bacon, chopped	1	teaspoon Dijon mustard
2	tablespoons butter	¼	teaspoon salt
½	red onion, finely chopped	¼	teaspoon freshly grated nutmeg
2	tablespoons unbleached all-purpose flour	2	hard-cooked eggs, peeled and coarsely chopped

In a covered saucepan, heat 1" of water to boiling. Place the spinach in a steamer basket and insert into the saucepan. Cook the spinach until thoroughly wilted. Allow to cool. Using your hands, squeeze all excess juice out of the spinach. (When using frozen spinach, thaw in a colander and squeeze off excess water.) Place the spinach on a cutting board and coarsely chop it. Set aside in a bowl.

In a medium saucepan over medium-low heat, cook the bacon until crispy. Drain on paper towels. Pour off the bacon fat and wipe out the pan. Return the pan to the heat and melt the butter. Add the onion and cook until softened. Stir in the flour and cook for 2 minutes, or until the mixture bubbles. Gradually whisk in the milk. Simmer, stirring frequently, over medium-low heat for 4 to 5 minutes, or until thickened.

Stir in the mustard, salt, and nutmeg. Allow to sit for 5 minutes. To serve, pour over the spinach and top with the bacon and eggs.

Makes 4 servings

Per serving: 208 calories, 12 g protein, 9 g carbohydrates, 14 g fat, 135 mg cholesterol, 10 g fiber, 466 mg sodium

SNAP BEAN, TOMATO, AND CORN SALAD

1	large ear corn	3	tablespoons balsamic vinegar
¾	pound green and/or yellow snap beans (green and/or wax beans), trimmed and cut into 2" pieces	¼	cup sliced fresh basil leaves
		1	can (2 ounces) anchovies, drained (optional)
2	tablespoons extra virgin olive oil	1	cup cherry tomatoes, halved
			Salt
½	red onion, thinly sliced		Freshly ground black pepper
2	garlic cloves, thinly sliced		

The medley of color and flavor in this salad is the epitome of late-summer produce. I like it as a side dish or tossed with pasta and shellfish as an entrée.

Bring a medium pot of lightly salted water to a boil. Cut the kernels from the ear of corn. Drop the beans into the boiling water for 1 to 2 minutes, or until tender-crisp. Add the corn kernels and cook for 10 seconds longer. Drain.

Heat the oil in a large skillet over medium heat. Add the onion and garlic and cook for 5 minutes, or until soft. Remove from the heat and add the vinegar, basil, and anchovies, if using.

Add the bean mixture and tomatoes, return to the heat, and cook for 1 minute to warm the tomatoes. Season with salt and pepper to taste.

Makes 6 servings

Per serving: 109 calories, 5 g protein, 11 g carbohydrates, 6 g fat, 8 mg cholesterol, 3 g fiber, 351 mg sodium

MASHED POTATO–STUFFED PEPPERS

This dish was created for a class I taught at Draeger's Culinary Center in Menlo Park, California. It literally made people smack their lips. I believe it was the creamy, luscious flavor of the combination of mashed potatoes and roasted peppers.

4	medium poblano or Anaheim chile peppers	1	pound all-purpose potatoes, peeled and cut into large chunks
2	garlic cloves, minced		
2	tablespoons red wine vinegar	2	tablespoons chopped fresh chives
1	tablespoon extra virgin olive oil	4	ounces cream cheese
½	teaspoon salt	¼–½	cup milk
¼	teaspoon freshly ground black pepper	½	cup (2 ounces) Cheddar or Monterey Jack cheese, shredded

Preheat the oven to 375°F.

Cut the chile peppers in half lengthwise, removing the seeds and stems and scraping away most of the white membranes.

In a medium bowl, combine the garlic, vinegar, oil, salt, and black pepper. Toss the chile peppers in the bowl to thoroughly coat. Place, cut side down, on a baking sheet and bake for 20 to 30 minutes, or until the peppers are tender.

Meanwhile, bring a large pot of salted water to a boil and cook the potatoes for 15 minutes, or until tender. Drain and place in a large bowl. Mash the potatoes with the chives. Cut the cream cheese into pieces and add to the potatoes, allowing it to melt and mash with the potatoes. Add enough milk as you are mashing to make the potatoes smooth and creamy.

Turn the peppers cut side up on the baking sheet. Mound the mashed potatoes in the baked peppers. Top with the shredded cheese. Bake for 15 minutes, or until lightly browned.

Makes 8 servings

Per serving: 145 calories, 5 g protein, 11 g carbohydrates, 9 g fat, 24 mg cholesterol, 1 g fiber, 532 mg sodium

RADICCHIO, ARUGULA, AND GOAT CHEESE SALAD

2	shallots, thinly sliced	¼	teaspoon salt
1	large garlic clove, minced	¼	teaspoon freshly ground black pepper
3	tablespoons olive oil		
3	tablespoons sherry wine vinegar	2	heads radicchio
2	tablespoons sugar	1	large bunch arugula
2	tablespoons finely chopped fresh Italian parsley	6	ounces soft goat cheese (such as chèvre)

I love to grow radicchio in my garden. The bitter leaves tossed with the arugula and goat cheese fill this a salad with robust flavors.

In a medium bowl, whisk together the shallots, garlic, oil, vinegar, sugar, parsley, salt, and pepper.

Add the radicchio and arugula and toss to coat. Allow to sit for 3 to 4 minutes, then break the goat cheese into bite-size pieces over the salad. Toss again and divide among 6 salad plates.

Makes 6 servings

Per serving: 169 calories, 6 g protein, 7 g carbohydrates, 13 g fat, 13 mg cholesterol, 1g fiber, 215 mg sodium

ASIAN CHICKEN SALAD

Chicken salads are extremely popular these days. By infusing bold flavors such as ginger and Chinese mustard, the need for oil is greatly diminished, and a delicious salad is enhanced.

½ cup seasoned rice wine vinegar

3 tablespoons soy sauce

1 teaspoon toasted sesame oil

1–2 tablespoons prepared hot Chinese mustard

2 tablespoons minced fresh ginger

2 green onions, thinly sliced

3 boneless, skinless chicken breast halves, sliced into ¼" strips

2 cups bean sprouts

1 red bell pepper, thinly sliced

6 cups shredded Savoy cabbage

1 tablespoon toasted sesame seeds

Preheat the oven to 400°F. Lightly oil a baking sheet.

In a large measuring cup, whisk together the vinegar, soy sauce, oil, mustard, ginger, and green onions. Pour half the dressing into a medium bowl.

Add the chicken to the bowl. Toss to coat and marinate for 10 minutes.

Meanwhile, in a large bowl, combine the sprouts, pepper, and cabbage. Toss with the remaining dressing. Allow to sit at room temperature for 20 minutes, tossing occasionally.

Place the chicken on the prepared baking sheet and bake for 10 minutes, or until cooked and no longer pink. Cool slightly, then add to the bowl with the cabbage mixture. Sprinkle with the sesame seeds.

Makes 4 servings

Per serving: 185 calories, 25 g protein, 14 g carbohydrates, 4 g fat, 51 mg cholesterol, 5 g fiber, 912 mg sodium

FRISÉE WITH SPICY MAPLE PECANS

1	cup pecans halves		2	tablespoons extra virgin olive oil
¼	cup pure maple syrup		2	ounces feta cheese, crumbled
½	teaspoon freshly ground black pepper		2–3	tablespoons red wine vinegar
½	teaspoon ground red pepper (optional)		½	tablespoon sugar
½	teaspoon salt		1	teaspoon Dijon mustard
1	garlic clove		2	medium heads frisée, cut into bite-size pieces
¼	red onion, chopped			

Preheat the oven to 400°F. Lightly oil a baking sheet.

In a small bowl, combine the pecans with the maple syrup. Sprinkle with the black pepper, red pepper (if using), and salt. Toss to coat well. Place in a single layer on the prepared baking sheet. Bake the nuts, tossing frequently, for 5 minutes, or until lightly toasted. Place on a rack to cool.

In a food processor or blender, combine the garlic and onion. Gradually add the oil and puree just until blended. Add the cheese, vinegar, sugar, and mustard and puree until well-blended. Place in a serving bowl.

Mound the frisée on each of 6 individual plates. Top with the nuts. Serve the dressing on the side.

Makes 6 servings

Per serving: 233 calories, 3 g protein, 15 g carbohydrates, 19 g fat, 8 mg cholesterol, 3 g fiber, 118 mg sodium

This interesting salad is wonderful as a first course, side dish, or served as a bed beneath grilled chicken or roasted game hen.

(photograph on page 158)

Alice Waters

Chez Panisse, **Berkeley, California**

Franklin Avery/Chez Panisse Café

We all know that making the decision to buy organic food is an ethical choice. But we have to concentrate on the next step, too, and that is teaching people to eat together. It's not just the food, it's what we do with it. If we are going to eat ethically, we had better start eating together with each other and our children. When you eat together, and eat a meal that you cooked by yourself, you are involved with the process in a different way. You shelled the peas, you peeled the potatoes, and you want everyone to enjoy every last bite. These are the kind of meals that we should be eating with our children.

AVOCADO AND BEET SALAD WITH CITRUS VINAIGRETTE

6	medium red or golden beets
	Salt and pepper
1	tablespoon red wine vinegar
	Extra virgin olive oil
1	large shallot, diced fine
2	tablespoons white wine vinegar

1	tablespoon lemon juice
1	tablespoon orange juice
	Chervil sprigs
¼	teaspoon chopped lemon zest
¼	teaspoon chopped orange zest
2	firm ripe avocados

Preheat the oven to 400°F.

Trim and wash the beets. Put them in a baking dish, add a splash of water, and cover tightly. Roast the beets in the oven for about 45 minutes until cooked through.

When the beets are cooked, allow them to cool uncovered. Peel and cut them into wedges. Place them in a bowl and season generously with salt and pepper. Add the red wine vinegar and 1 tablespoon of olive oil. Toss gently.

Place the shallot in a bowl and add the white wine vinegar, lemon juice, orange juice, and a pinch of salt. Let macerate for 15 minutes.

Makes 6 servings

Whisk in ¾ cup oil and stir in the chopped chervil, lemon zest, and orange zest. Taste for seasoning.

Cut the avocados in half lengthwise and remove the pits. Leaving the skin intact, cut the avocados lengthwise into ¼" slices. Scoop out the slices with a large spoon and arrange them on a platter or individual dishes. Season with salt and pepper. Arrange the beets over the avocado slices and drizzle with the vinaigrette. Garnish with a few chervil sprigs.

APPLESAUCE OATMEAL COOKIES

1 cup whole grain pastry flour

1 teaspoon baking powder

¾ teaspoon salt

½ teaspoon ground cinnamon

½ cup butter, softened

1 cup packed brown sugar

1 egg

½ cup applesauce

¾ teaspoon vanilla extract

2 cups oats

½ cup raisins (optional)

¼ cup ground walnuts or pecans (optional)

The applesauce in this recipe keeps the cookies moist, just like it does in applesauce cake.

Preheat the oven to 375°F. Line a baking sheet with parchment paper.

In medium bowl, combine the flour, baking powder, salt, and cinnamon. Set aside.

In a large bowl with an electric mixer on medium speed, beat the butter and brown sugar until light and fluffy. Add the egg, applesauce, and vanilla extract.

Gradually combine the flour mixture with the egg mixture. Stir in the oats, raisins, and nuts, if using.

Drop by large teaspoonfuls onto the prepared baking sheet. Bake for 10 minutes, or until lightly browned.

Makes 36

Per cookie: 106 calories, 2 g protein, 15 g carbohydrates, 4 g fat, 13 mg cholesterol, 1 g fiber, 64 mg sodium

UPSIDE-DOWN PEAR CHOCOLATE CAKE

1¾	cups whole grain pastry flour		2	eggs
1¾	cups sugar		¾	cup brewed strong coffee, cooled
¾	cup unsweetened cocoa powder		¾	cup buttermilk
2	teaspoons baking soda		½	cup vegetable oil
1	teaspoon baking powder		1	teaspoon vanilla extract
¾	teaspoon salt		2–3	large pears, peeled, cored, and sliced

Preheat the oven to 375°F. Lightly oil a 10" cake pan. Line the pan with parchment or waxed paper and lightly oil the paper.

In a medium bowl, combine the flour, sugar, cocoa, baking soda, baking powder, and salt.

In large bowl, whisk together the eggs, coffee, buttermilk, oil, and vanilla extract. Gradually stir the flour mixture into the egg mixture. Mix until thoroughly blended.

Line the bottom of the cake pan with the pears in a circular design. Pour the batter on top of the pears. Bake for 55 minutes, or until a wooden pick inserted in the center comes out clean.

Place on a rack and let stand for 10 minutes. With a butter knife, cut around the edge of the cake, loosening the sides. Invert the pan onto a plate. Using the handle of the knife, vigorously tap the top of the pan, even shaking it a bit, to loosen the cake. Leave the pan over the cake for 15 minutes. Remove the pan and let the cake cool completely.

Makes 10 servings

Per serving: 323 calories, 5 g protein, 52 g carbohydrates, 11 g fat, 36 mg cholesterol, 2 g fiber, 385 mg sodium

My favorite desserts are custards, puddings, pies, and tarts. When custard is baked in a pie, it often makes the crust soggy. When I make this dessert, the custard and crust are created separately and assembled just before serving.

COCONUT CUSTARD TARTLETS

Crusts

1	cup cold unsalted butter	½	teaspoon ground nutmeg
2½–3	cups whole grain pastry flour	¾	teaspoon salt
		6–10	tablespoons milk

Custard

8	large egg yolks	½	whole vanilla bean
¾	cup sugar	1½	cups unsweetened coconut, toasted
	Pinch of salt		
3	tablespoons cornstarch	3	tablespoons unsalted butter
2½	cups whole milk		

To make the crusts: Preheat the oven to 425°F.

In a medium bowl, combine 2½ cups of the flour, nutmeg, and salt. Grate the butter into the mixture. Using your hands or a pastry blender, cut the butter into the flour mixture. Gradually add the milk to the flour mixture, blending it together to just form a dough.

Divide the dough into 12 pieces and roll them into small balls. On a well-floured board, flatten them into disks and roll into 8" circles, adding plenty of flour until firm. Place in twelve 4" tart shells with removable bottoms. Or, using your hands, roll the outer edges 2 small turns toward the middle to form an edge.

Place the tart shells on a baking sheet. (If making free-form shells, line the sheet with parchment paper. Bake for 15 minutes, or until lightly browned. Remove to a rack to cool.

To make the custard: Meanwhile, in a medium bowl, whisk together the egg yolks, sugar, salt, and cornstarch. Place the milk and vanilla bean in a medium saucepan. Bring to a simmer over medium heat and slowly whisk in the egg mixture. Stir in 1¼ cups of the coconut, reserving the rest for garnish.

Cook the mixture over medium heat, stirring constantly, for 10 minutes, or until thickened. Remove the saucepan from the heat. Remove and discard the vanilla bean. Whisk in the butter.

Place the coconut custard in a bowl. Cover with waxed paper and refrigerate for 2 hours, or until chilled.

To serve, fill the shells with the custard. Sprinkle with the remaining ¼ cup coconut.

Makes 12 servings

Per serving: 438 calories, 8 g protein, 39 g carbohydrates, 28 g fat, 201 mg cholesterol, 1 g fiber, 217 mg sodium

AUTUMN HARVEST

I don't need a calendar to alert me when autumn arrives. I know it on my daily walks, when the mornings are cold and the fallen leaves crunch beneath my feet. Inside, my bare feet are now covered with socks, and the closed windows get steamy as the cold outdoors collides with the warmth from my kitchen.

At the farmers' market, the availability of fresh produce has dwindled. Even in your own garden, you might be lucky enough to find remnants of summer crops, perhaps a few tomatoes still clinging to a vine or a handful of raspberries. This is the time when fall crops hit their prime in color, taste, and texture. Squash, pumpkins, cabbage, tangerines, apples, pomegranates, and persimmons are treasured.

During autumn, I try to use every fresh ingredient available, orchestrating them with preserved foods such as organic canned, dried, or frozen fruits and vegetables. As always, I do my best to use what grows as close to my home as possible or willingly pay the extra for organic and pesticide-free produce grown elsewhere.

Night falls faster, almost giving license to cook more. I enjoy creating robust dishes, indulging myself in bone-sticking, rich foods that protect me from the cold. I relish the challenge of cutting a rebellious winter squash or figuring creative ways to use parsnips and celery root.

Again, autumn is the time to reach for dried, canned, and frozen ingredients from your pantry shelves and freezer. Satisfy your hunger for a tomato dish by using ones that you canned, dried, or froze a few months ago.

KITCHEN TIP

I like to make soups a day or two ahead for the flavors to meld perfectly. Try making some on the weekend and refrigerate until later in the week for a speedy supper. Don't forget a tossed salad and crusty bread.

CREAMY AUTUMN SOUP

2 tablespoons butter

1 medium onion, finely chopped

½ cup dry white wine

5 cups chicken broth

1 large russet potato, peeled and chopped

1 large celery root (celeriac), about 1 pound, peeled and chopped

1½ tablespoons chopped fresh thyme

1 cup heavy cream

1 apple, peeled and chopped into ¼" pieces

Salt

Freshly ground black pepper

1 cup (4 ounces) shredded Cheddar or Jarlsberg cheese

In a large pot over medium-high heat, melt the butter and cook the onion for 4 minutes, or until soft. Add the wine and cook for 3 minutes longer. Add the broth, potato, celery root, and thyme. Bring to a boil over high heat. Reduce the heat to medium-low, cover, and simmer for 1 hour, or until the vegetables are very soft.

Working in batches if necessary, place the mixture in a food processor or blender. Process until smooth. Add the cream and pulse just until blended. Stir in the apple and season with salt and pepper to taste.

Top with the cheese.

Makes 6 servings

Per serving: 322 calories, 8 g protein, 15 g carbohydrates, 25 g fat, 86 mg cholesterol, 3 g fiber, 657 mg sodium

BROCCOLI AND GINGER DUMPLINGS

4	tablespoons soy sauce	1½	cups finely chopped fresh or thawed frozen broccoli
2	tablespoons brown sugar	1	cup vegetable or chicken broth
½	teaspoon toasted sesame oil	1	garlic clove, minced
3	tablespoons rice wine vinegar	1	tablespoon grated fresh ginger
½	teaspoon red-pepper flakes	24	round wonton wrappers
1	tablespoon olive oil	2	green onions, thinly sliced
1	small red onion, grated	1	teaspoon black sesame seeds (optional)

In a small bowl, combine 3 tablespoons of the soy sauce, the brown sugar, sesame oil, vinegar, and red-pepper flakes; set aside.

Bring a large skillet of salted water to a boil over high heat. Reduce the heat to low, cover, and simmer.

Heat the olive oil in a large skillet over medium heat. Add the red onion and cook for 2 minutes, or until soft. Add the broccoli and broth. Cover and cook for 10 minutes, or until the broccoli is very soft and all the broth has evaporated. Add the garlic, ginger, and the remaining 1 tablespoon soy sauce; cook for 2 minutes. Drain off any excess liquid and cool.

Place 1 teaspoon of broccoli filling in the center of each wonton wrapper. Moisten the outer edges of each wrapper with water and tightly seal using a wonton press or your fingers.

Working in batches if necessary, place the wontons into the simmering water for 2 minutes, or until heated through. Drain and place on a platter with the dipping sauce. Sprinkle with the green onions and sesame seeds.

Makes 6 servings

Per serving: 165 calories, 6 g protein, 27 g carbohydrates, 4 g fat, 3 mg cholesterol, 2 g fiber, 1,048 mg sodium

ONION-HOMINY DIP

1 tablespoon olive oil

1 small red onion, finely chopped

¾ cup canned hominy, drained

1–2 garlic cloves, minced

⅛–¼ teaspoon ground red pepper

⅓ cup finely chopped fresh cilantro

1 cup sour cream

½ cup buttermilk

2 tablespoons chopped fresh chives or green onion

Salt

Heat the oil in a medium skillet over medium heat. Add the onion and cook for 6 minutes, or until very soft. Add the hominy, garlic, and pepper. Cook for 3 minutes longer.

Cool slightly and place in a medium bowl. Add the cilantro, sour cream, buttermilk, and chives or green onion, stirring until well-blended. Season with salt to taste. Allow to stand for 30 minutes before serving.

Makes 8 servings

Per serving: 90 calories, 2 g protein, 5 g carbohydrates, 7 g fat, 11 mg cholesterol, 1 g fiber, 62 mg sodium

The hominy in this dip adds texture and flavor. I like to make vegetable chips for dipping. Using a mandolin or sharp knife, slice off thin rounds from raw, peeled beets, parsnips, carrots, or turnips. Serve with the dip along with organic potato chips.

KITCHEN TIPS

If you don't like hominy, use an equal amount of drained, canned chopped tomatoes. Also, ¼ teaspoon ground red pepper makes this dip quite spicy. Use less if you prefer your dips more mild. Taste and adjust accordingly.

ROAST CHICKEN WITH CRANBERRY-ALMOND STUFFING

Chicken

1	roasting chicken (3 to 4 pounds)	¼	teaspoon freshly ground black pepper
1	tablespoon olive oil	2	teaspoons paprika
¼	teaspoon salt		

Stuffing

3	tablespoons butter	1½	pounds hearty whole grain or semolina bread, broken into pieces
2	celery ribs, chopped		
1	onion, chopped	2	eggs, beaten
4	ounces mushrooms, sliced	2–3	cups chicken broth
1	tablespoon ground sage	½	teaspoon salt
⅓	cup slivered almonds, chopped	¼	teaspoon freshly ground black pepper
⅓	cup dried cranberries or cherries		

Preheat the oven to 475°F. Lightly butter a 2-quart baking dish.

To make the chicken: Rub the chicken with the oil and season with the salt, pepper, and paprika. Place on a rack in a roasting pan and roast for 20 minutes. Reduce the heat to 375°F and continue roasting for 1 hour, or until a thermometer inserted in a breast registers 180°F and the juices run clear. Let stand for 10 minutes before carving.

To make the stuffing: Meanwhile, melt the butter in a medium skillet over medium-high heat. Add the celery, onion, and mushrooms and cook for 5 minutes, or until soft. Add the sage, almonds, and cranberries or cherries and cook for 1 minute. Remove from the heat.

Place the bread in a large bowl and toss with the mushroom mixture. Add the eggs, stirring to blend well. Add 2 cups of the broth, salt, and pepper; stir well. Add the remaining 1 cup broth if a moister stuffing is preferred. Place in the prepared baking dish.

Add to the oven during the last 30 minutes of the chicken roasting time. Bake for 30 minutes, or until the stuffing puffs up and the top is light brown.

Makes 6 servings

Per serving: 551 calories, 42 g protein, 45 g carbohydrates, 24 g fat, 161 mg cholesterol, 7 g fiber, 1,050 mg sodium

---

I prefer to roast my stuffing separately from the bird. It lessens the possibility of overcooking the meat and produces a crisp, dense stuffing. Since the stuffing is my favorite part of this dish anyway, sometimes I don't even bother with the chicken!

KITCHEN TIP

This recipe works great for Thanksgiving. To roast a turkey, double the chicken seasonings and prepare as you would the chicken. Roast a 12- to 14-pound bird for 3 to 3½ hours, or until a thermometer inserted in a breast registers 180°F and the juices run clear. Let stand for 10 minutes before carving. Prepare the stuffing as directed, doubling if necessary.

If you can get your butcher to bone the chicken thighs, then this recipe can be prepared and on the table within 30 minutes. These chicken thighs are delicious served over hearty grains such as barley or brown rice.

KITCHEN TIP

If you choose not to eat the skin of the thighs, you will reduce the fat by 23 grams and the calories by 195.

CHÈVRE-STUFFED CHICKEN THIGHS

4	ounces soft goat cheese (such as chèvre)	½	teaspoon freshly ground black pepper
¼	cup currants or raisins	1	tablespoon olive oil
2	tablespoons bread crumbs	1	tablespoon mixed dried Italian herbs
1	tablespoon chopped fresh chives	½	teaspoon salt
1	tablespoon chopped fresh oregano or 1 teaspoon dried	8	chicken thighs

Preheat the oven to 400°F.

In a small bowl, combine the cheese, currants or raisins, bread crumbs, chives, oregano, and pepper.

In another small bowl, combine the oil, Italian herbs, and salt.

Place the chicken on a rack in a roasting pan. Lift the skin of each thigh and place one-eighth of the cheese mixture under the skin. Brush the skin with the oil mixture.

Roast for 30 minutes, or until a thermometer inserted in the thickest portion registers 170°F and the juices run clear.

Makes 4 servings

Per serving: 545 calories, 38 g protein, 10 g carbohydrates, 38 g fat, 171 mg cholesterol, 2 g fiber, 547 mg sodium

SHORT RIBS WITH BEETS

3	pounds beef short ribs		4	sprigs fresh thyme
2	tablespoons garam masala		4	sprigs fresh Italian parsley
6	garlic cloves, chopped		2	bay leaves
8	shallots		2	teaspoons ground coriander
2	carrots, finely chopped		1	teaspoon ground cloves
2	celery ribs, finely chopped		1	teaspoon salt
1	cup hearty red wine (such as zinfandel)		1	teaspoon freshly ground black pepper
3–4	cups vegetable or chicken broth		6	beets, trimmed and scrubbed
1	can (14½ ounces) diced tomatoes			

Preheat the oven to 450°F.

Season the ribs with the garam masala and a pinch of salt and pepper. Place in a large roasting pan and roast for 45 minutes, or until the meat is browned.

Reduce the heat to 375°F. Add the garlic, shallots, carrots, celery, wine, 3 cups of the broth, tomatoes (with juice), thyme, parsley, bay leaves, coriander, cloves, salt, and pepper. Roast, uncovered, for 1½ hours, or until the meat is tender but not yet falling off the bone.

Cut the beets into large wedges and add to the ribs. Spoon the sauce over the beets and ribs. Add the remaining 1 cup broth if the sauce is too thick. Roast for 1 hour, or until the beets and meat are tender.

Using tongs or a slotted spoon, remove the ribs and beets to a serving platter.

Remove and discard the bay leaves and any sprigs in the sauce. Working in batches if necessary, place the sauce in a food processor or blender. Puree until smooth.

Pour the sauce over the ribs and beets.

Makes 6 servings

Per serving: 581 calories, 53 g protein, 21 g carbohydrates, 25 g fat, 109 mg cholesterol, 5 g fiber, 1,139 mg sodium

Once you begin cooking with meats that are not treated with artificial hormones or antibiotics, you will notice a difference in flavor. I find that organic meats have much more flavor than conventional ones.

PORK CHOPS WITH CHERRY PORT SAUCE

Reminiscent of the old-fashioned pork and cherry glaze, this rich sauce is a delicious balance to flavorful pork chops. For a change of pace, try the sauce over smoked pork chops or even ham steak.

3	whole cloves or ½ teaspoon ground cloves	1	cup ruby port
3	whole black peppercorns	1	cup water
1	bay leaf	3	tablespoons brown sugar
1	cinnamon stick	1	tablespoon Dijon mustard
1½	cups dried cherries	2	tablespoons butter
		4	pork rib chops

Place the cloves, peppercorns, bay leaf, and cinnamon stick in cheesecloth or a small gauze bag. Tie with kitchen twine to seal. Place in a medium saucepan along with the cherries, port, water, brown sugar, and mustard. Bring to a boil over high heat. Reduce the heat to low and simmer for 1 hour, or until the liquid is reduced by half and thickened slightly. Remove and discard the spice bag.

Melt the butter in a large skillet over medium-high heat. Add the chops and cook for 8 minutes, turning once, or until a thermometer inserted in the center of a chop registers 160°F and the juices run clear.

Serve with the sauce.

Makes 4 servings

Per serving: 548 calories, 21 g protein, 76 g carbohydrates, 14 g fat, 69 mg cholesterol, 1 g fiber, 152 mg sodium

Pork Chops with Cherry Port Sauce and Barley–Sweet Potato Hash (page 195)

SPAGHETTI SQUASH WITH CLAM SAUCE

1   spaghetti squash (about 1½ pounds)

2   tablespoons extra virgin olive oil

2   tablespoons unsalted butter

2   large garlic cloves, minced

1   can (2 ounces) anchovies, drained and chopped

2   tablespoons capers

1   tablespoon lemon zest

36 clams (such as littleneck, manilla, or cherrystone), scrubbed

1   bottle (8 ounces) clam juice

½   cup dry vermouth

1–2 teaspoons red-pepper flakes (optional)

2   tablespoons chopped fresh parsley

    Salt

    Freshly ground black pepper

¼   cup (1 ounce) grated Asiago, Romano, or Parmesan cheese

Preheat the oven to 375°F. Cut the squash in half lengthwise. Scrape out and discard the seeds. Place the squash, cut side down, in a heavy baking dish and add 1 cup water. Bake for 35 minutes, or until tender. Cool slightly.

When cool, using a fork, scrape crosswise to pull the strands of squash away from the shell. Place in a large bowl.

Meanwhile, heat the oil and butter in a large skillet over medium heat. Add the garlic, anchovies, capers, and lemon zest. Cook, stirring frequently, for 5 minutes.

While the squash is cooling, add the clams, clam juice, and vermouth to the skillet with the garlic mixture. Place over high heat and bring to a boil. Reduce the heat to low, cover, and simmer for 5 minutes, or until the clams open. Discard any unopened clams. Add the red-pepper flakes, if using, and parsley and season with salt and pepper to taste. Pour over the spaghetti squash.

Sprinkle with the cheese.

Makes 4 servings

Per serving: 327 calories, 19 g protein, 16 g carbohydrates, 18 g fat, 62 mg cholesterol, 2 g fiber, 909 mg sodium

Spaghetti squash has a wonderful texture. The cooked strands look like spaghetti and seem to hold up well under any sauce that you might use with pasta. This sauce is also good served over other winter squash such as butternut or acorn.

MEDITERRANEAN STUFFED WHITEFISH

2 tablespoons extra virgin olive oil

1 small red onion, finely chopped

2 garlic cloves, minced

2 large bunches fresh spinach, chopped, or 1 package (10 ounces) frozen chopped spinach, thawed and squeezed dry

1 tablespoon chopped fresh oregano

1 tablespoon chopped fresh mint

2 tablespoons pine nuts

4 ounces feta cheese, crumbled

4 mild whitefish fillets (about 1½ pounds), such as sole, flounder, cod, halibut

Juice of 1½ lemons

Salt

Freshly ground black pepper

Preheat the oven to 400°F. Coat a large baking dish with oil.

Heat the oil in a medium skillet over medium heat. Add the onion and cook for 4 minutes, or until soft. Add the garlic and cook for 1 minute longer. Add the spinach and cook, stirring constantly, for 3 minutes longer, or until wilted. Remove from the heat and stir in the oregano, mint, pine nuts, and cheese. Cool slightly.

Place the fish in the prepared baking dish. Spoon one-quarter of the spinach mixture onto the center of each fillet and fold the fish in half. Drizzle the lemon juice over the fish. Season with salt and pepper to taste.

Bake for 15 to 20 minutes, or until the fish flakes easily.

Makes 4 servings
Per serving: 329 calories, 42 g protein, 15 g carbohydrates, 18 g fat, 67 mg cholesterol, 5 g fiber, 474 mg sodium

WILD, WILD PASTA

<table>
<tr><td>1</td><td>pound fettuccine</td></tr>
<tr><td>¼</td><td>cup extra virgin olive oil</td></tr>
<tr><td>2</td><td>garlic cloves, minced</td></tr>
<tr><td>1–2</td><td>jalapeño chile peppers, seeded and finely chopped</td></tr>
<tr><td>¼</td><td>cup dry white wine</td></tr>
<tr><td>8</td><td>ounces wild mushrooms (such as chanterelle, black trumpet, lobster, or porcini)</td></tr>
<tr><td>1½</td><td>cups cooked wild rice</td></tr>
<tr><td>6</td><td>ounces feta cheese, crumbled</td></tr>
<tr><td>½</td><td>cup coarsely chopped oil-packed sun-dried tomatoes, drained</td></tr>
<tr><td>2</td><td>tablespoons finely chopped fresh marjoram or 1 tablespoon dried</td></tr>
<tr><td>1</td><td>tablespoon lemon zest</td></tr>
<tr><td></td><td>Salt</td></tr>
<tr><td></td><td>Freshly ground black pepper</td></tr>
<tr><td></td><td>Chopped fresh parsley</td></tr>
</table>

This great cool-weather pasta is a favorite in my restaurant, Flea St. Café, reappearing each year as soon as the last of the fresh tomatoes disappear.

Cook the pasta according to package directions. Drain and place in a large bowl.

Meanwhile, heat the oil in a large skillet over medium heat. Add the garlic and chile pepper and cook for 1 minute. Add the wine and cook for 1 minute longer. Add the mushrooms and cook, stirring frequently, for 3 to 4 minutes, wilting the mushrooms slightly. Remove from the heat and stir in the rice, cheese, tomatoes, marjoram, and lemon zest. Season with salt and black pepper to taste.

Add the mushroom sauce to the pasta and toss to coat. Garnish with parsley.

Makes 8 servings

Per serving: 515 calories, 17 g protein, 67 g carbohydrates, 20 g fat, 95 mg cholesterol, 4 g fiber, 1,258 mg sodium

AUTUMN VEGETABLE GRATIN

¼ cup unbleached all-purpose flour

¼ cup brown sugar

1 cup (4 ounces) shredded Cheddar cheese

1 teaspoon salt

½ teaspoon freshly ground black pepper

1½ pounds winter squash (butternut, buttercup, Hokaido, or acorn), peeled and thinly sliced

1 onion, peeled and thinly sliced

2 golden flesh potatoes (such as Yukon gold), peeled and thinly sliced

1 fennel bulb, peeled and thinly sliced

2–3 cups milk

½ cup (2 ounces) grated Parmesan cheese

The thinner you slice the vegetables, the better. I use a tool called a mandolin, which is a small tabletop slicer. You can find it in most cookware shops or catalogs. Otherwise, use a very sharp knife, take your time, and you will get the same results.

Preheat oven to 350°F. Oil a 2-quart baking dish.

In a small bowl, combine the flour, brown sugar, Cheddar, salt, and pepper. Set aside.

Layer one-third of the squash, onion, potatoes, and fennel in the prepared baking dish. Dust with one-third of the flour mixture. Continue layering all 3 layers, finishing with the flour mixture. Pour the milk over all. Sprinkle with the Parmesan.

Bake for 1½ hours, or until the vegetables are very tender and the gratin is golden brown. If the top browns too quickly, cover loosely with foil. Let stand for 15 minutes before serving.

Makes 8 servings

Per serving: 245 calories, 11 g protein, 28 g carbohydrates, 11 g fat, 28 mg cholesterol, 3 g fiber, 547 mg sodium

KITCHEN TIP

For a lighter version of this luscious dish, use vegetable or chicken broth instead of milk. I like to make this dish the day before serving, as the flavors seem to improve.

ROASTED PARSNIPS

1 pound parsnips, peeled and cut into 3" × ½" sticks

2 tablespoons olive oil

1 teaspoon chopped fresh oregano

¼ teaspoon salt

¼ teaspoon freshly ground black pepper

Preheat the oven to 375°F. Line a baking sheet with parchment paper or foil.

Place the parsnips in a large bowl. Add the oil, oregano, salt, and pepper. Toss to coat well. Place on the prepared baking sheet.

Roast, turning occasionally, for 30 minutes, or until the parsnips are tender and lightly browned.

Makes 6 servings

Per serving: 99 calories, 1 g protein, 14 g carbohydrates, 5 g fat, 0 mg cholesterol, 4 g fiber, 105 mg sodium

SMOKY FRISÉE SALAD

Vinaigrette

1	cup cranberry sauce (chunky or smooth)	1	tablespoon orange zest
¼	cup extra virgin olive oil	3	large fresh mint leaves, finely chopped
1	tablespoon Dijon mustard	¼	teaspoon salt
3	tablespoons red wine vinegar	¼	teaspoon freshly ground black pepper
1	tablespoon water		

Croutons

6	ounces smoked Cheddar or firm smoked cheese	½	cup dried toasted bread crumbs
½	cup unbleached all-purpose flour	½	teaspoon salt
1	large egg	¼	teaspoon freshly ground black pepper
2	tablespoons cold water	3	small heads frisée

To make the vinaigrette: Place the cranberry sauce in a medium bowl and gradually whisk in the oil until smooth. Whisk in the mustard, vinegar, water, orange zest, mint, salt, and pepper. Set aside.

To make the croutons: Preheat the oven to 350°F. Lightly oil a baking sheet.

Cut the cheese into ½" squares.

Place the flour in a small bowl. In another small bowl, beat the egg with the water. On a piece of waxed paper, combine the bread crumbs, salt, and pepper.

Working in batches, toss the cheese in the flour, then in the egg, tossing to coat thoroughly. Toss the cheese in the bread crumb mixture to coat thoroughly. Place on the prepared baking sheet.

Bake for 8 minutes, or until lightly browned.

Place the frisée in a large bowl. Toss with the vinaigrette. Evenly divide among 6 salad plates. Top with the croutons.

Makes 6 servings

Per serving: 350 calories, 10 g protein, 34 g carbohydrates, 20 g fat, 65 mg cholesterol, 2 g fiber, 522 mg sodium

There are a handful of wonderful organic smoked cheeses on the market, so if you can't find Cheddar, any cheese—smoky or not—will work.

KITCHEN TIP

This vinaigrette is delicious for basting a turkey or chicken, and the drippings make a fabulous gravy.

TANGERINE SLAW WITH SALMON ROULADES

Slaw

½	cup tangerine or orange juice		1	teaspoon red-pepper flakes or 1 tablespoon chopped fresh chile pepper
¼	cup packed brown sugar			
2	tablespoons extra virgin olive oil		½	teaspoon salt
4	tablespoons finely chopped fresh chives		½	head red cabbage, sliced very thin (about 8 cups)

Roulades

4	ounces cream cheese, softened		¼	pound thinly sliced smoked salmon
1	tablespoon grated red onion		1	head butter or Boston lettuce
1	teaspoon chopped fresh thyme		2	tangerines, sectioned

To make the slaw: In a large bowl, whisk together the juice, brown sugar, oil, chives, red-pepper flakes or chile pepper, and salt. Add the cabbage and toss to coat. Cover and let stand at room temperature for 1 hour, tossing occasionally.

To make the roulades: Meanwhile, in a small bowl, combine the cream cheese, onion, and thyme.

Lay the salmon flat on a clean work surface. Spread the cream cheese mixture thinly over the salmon. Starting from a narrow end, tightly roll the salmon into roulades. Wrap tightly in plastic wrap and refrigerate for at least 45 minutes. Place the roulades on a cutting board and slice into ½" rounds.

To serve, evenly divide the lettuce among 6 plates. Top with the slaw. Arrange the roulades on top of the slaw. Garnish with the tangerine sections.

Makes 6 servings

Per serving: 192 calories, 7 g protein, 15 g carbohydrates, 12 g fat, 25 mg cholesterol, 4 g fiber, 420 mg sodium

PICKLED CAULIFLOWER

1 large cauliflower head (about 3 pounds), cut into florets

4 garlic cloves, smashed

1 jalapeño chile pepper, quartered and seeded

6 whole peppercorns

2 bay leaves

5 cups rice wine vinegar

Place 1" of water in a large saucepan over high heat. Place a steamer basket in the pan and bring to a boil. Place the cauliflower in the basket and steam for 4 minutes, or until tender-crisp. Place in a colander and run under cold water. Drain completely.

Meanwhile, evenly divide the garlic, chile pepper, peppercorns, and bay leaves among two 2-quart jars. Add the cauliflower and completely cover with vinegar. Cover and refrigerate for up to 3 weeks. Remove and discard the bay leaves before serving.

Makes 20 servings

Per serving: 19 calories, 1 g protein, 4 g carbohydrates, 0 g fat, 0 mg cholesterol, 1 g fiber, 127 mg sodium

I planted enough cauliflower in my winter garden to feed the neighborhood. By the end of the season, with three or four gigantic heads still staring me in the face, I decided to make these delicious cauliflower pickles.

John Ash

Fetzer Vineyards, Hopland, California

Courtesy of Fetzer Vineyards

My own interest in organics started with my restaurant in Sonoma County in the northern California wine country in the late 1970s. I was greatly influenced by the messages of Alice Waters and other cooks about the importance of organically grown foods. Initially, my interest was not politically or ecologically driven, but motivated more by the fact that organically grown food just tasted better. As I worked more with organic farmers, however, I began to see the importance of organic agriculture beyond simply superior taste.

ROASTED ROOT VEGETABLES SCENTED WITH APPLE AND MUSTARD

3   cups apple cider or juice

1   cup fruity white wine such as Fetzer Gewürztraminer

2   tablespoons smooth Dijon mustard

3   tablespoons butter

4–5   pounds root vegetables, both sweet (carrots, parsnips, and/or yams) and savory (turnips, rutabagas and/or celery root), peeled and cut into ½" cubes

Salt and freshly ground pepper

In a saucepan, reduce the apple cider or juice, wine, and mustard over high heat to 1½ cups. Whisk in the butter and pour over the vegetables, tossing to coat. Season with salt and pepper and place the vegetables in a single layer in a large roasting pan(s) in a preheated 375° oven. Roast for 1 hour or so, or until the vegetables are lightly browned and tender. Stir the vegetables 3 or 4 times during the roasting process to promote browning on all sides.

Makes 8 servings

BARLEY–SWEET POTATO HASH

½ cup pearl barley

2 tablespoons vegetable or light olive oil

1 small onion, coarsely chopped

1 sweet potato, peeled and cut into ¼" pieces

2 cups vegetable broth

Salt

Freshly ground black pepper

Place the barley in a medium saucepan over medium heat. Cook, shaking the pan often, for 5 minutes, or until toasted. Remove the barley to a bowl.

In the same saucepan, heat the oil over medium heat. Add the onion and sweet potato and cook, stirring occasionally, for 5 minutes, or until lightly browned.

Add the barley and broth. Bring to a boil over high heat. Reduce the heat to medium-low, cover, and simmer, stirring occasionally, for 30 minutes, or until the barley is tender but still firm and the liquid is absorbed. Season generously with salt and pepper.

Makes 4 servings
Per serving: 209 calories, 4 g protein, 33 g carbohydrates, 7 g fat, 0 mg cholesterol, 6 g fiber, 158 mg sodium

Next to my organic raised beds is a coop with eight chickens, who give me the best eggs in the world! I make this hash and top it with a couple of those fresh eggs, poached or fried over easy. The yolks seep into the hash, and the only thing left to reach for is the bottle of hot sauce.

(photograph on page 183)

KITCHEN TIP

I like to stir ham, smoked tofu, or cooked chicken or shrimp into a bowl of this hash to make a hearty meal.

Vanilla ice cream or warm
vanilla custard are dreamy
with this hearty dessert. In
earnest, I like it best the next
day for breakfast next to a cup
of steaming hot English
breakfast tea.

PUMPKIN-RAISIN BREAD PUDDING

1 medium Cinderella pumpkin (about 7 to 8 pounds)

6 tablespoons unsalted butter, melted

¾ cup packed brown sugar

1 teaspoon ground cinnamon

¼ cup pure maple syrup

1 loaf (¾ pound) dense white bread, such as Italian, challah, or English muffin bread

¾ cup golden raisins

½ cup chopped walnuts or pecans

2 cups whole milk

3 eggs

1 cup (4 ounces) shredded Cheddar cheese

Preheat the oven to 375°F. Cut the top off the pumpkin. Clean out the seeds and scrape out the stringy membranes; discard.

In a small bowl, combine the butter, brown sugar, cinnamon, and maple syrup. Brush the inside of the pumpkin with 1 tablespoon of the butter mixture. Place on a baking sheet and bake for 45 minutes, or until tender when pierced with a fork.

Meanwhile, break the bread into bite-size pieces and place in a large bowl with the raisins and nuts. Pour the remaining butter mixture over the bread and toss to coat well.

In a measuring cup, whisk together the milk, eggs, and cheese.

When the pumpkin is tender, remove it from the oven and carefully fill it with the bread mixture. Top with the egg mixture. Push the ingredients down so that everything gets soaked in the liquid.

Return to the oven and bake for 1 hour, or until the pudding puffs up at the center and a knife inserted near the center comes out clean. Place on a rack and cool for at least 30 minutes. Slice into wedges to serve.

Makes 10 servings

Per serving: 390 calories, 10 g protein, 57 g carbohydrates, 15 g fat, 90 mg cholesterol, 9 g fiber, 124 mg sodium

MY FAVORITE NUT PIE

Crust

1	cup whole grain pastry flour	½	cup unsalted butter
1	teaspoon sugar	1	teaspoon red wine vinegar
½	teaspoon salt	½	cup ice water

Filling

2	tablespoon butter, softened	2	teaspoons vanilla extract
½	cup packed brown sugar	1½	cups mixed nuts, coarsely chopped (such pistachios, walnuts, pecans, pine nuts, almonds, cashews, hazelnuts)
1	cup light corn syrup		
3	eggs		
1½	teaspoons cornstarch		

To make the crust: In a large bowl, combine the flour, sugar, and salt. Grate the butter into the mixture. Using your hands or a pastry blender, work the butter into the flour mixture until the pieces are about the size of peas.

In a small bowl, combine the vinegar and water. Add to the flour mixture, 1 tablespoon at a time, and blend until a soft, moist dough is formed. It should be somewhat sticky.

Form the dough into a ball, then flatten into a round disk. Wrap in plastic wrap and refrigerate for at least 1 hour.

When the dough is chilled, place it on a well-floured surface and roll to about a ⅛" thickness, turning and flouring the dough often to keep it well-floured. Fold the dough in half and place in a 9" or 10" pie plate. Turn under and crimp the crust. Refrigerate.

To make the filling: Preheat oven to 375°F.

In a large bowl, with an electric mixer on medium speed, beat the butter, brown sugar, and corn syrup until well-blended. Add the eggs, cornstarch, and vanilla extract and beat until smooth.

Scatter the nuts into the chilled pie crust. Top with the egg mixture.

Bake for 45 minutes, or until a knife inserted near the center comes out clean. Cool completely before serving.

Makes 10 servings

Per serving: 413 calories, 7 g protein, 47 g carbohydrates, 24 g fat, 97 mg cholesterol, 2 g fiber, 180 mg sodium

PERSIMMON-BERRY CRISP

Topping

2 cups whole grain pastry flour

2 cups rolled oats

2 teaspoons ground cinnamon

½ teaspoon ground cloves

½ cup butter, softened slightly and cut into pieces

Persimmon Mixture

8 Fuyu persimmons, peeled and cut into thin wedges

2 pints red raspberries

½ cup sugar

3 tablespoons butter

To make the topping: Preheat the oven to 350°F. Butter a 3-quart baking dish.

In a medium bowl, combine the flour, oats, cinnamon, and cloves. Using your hands or a pastry blender, work the butter into the flour mixture until the pieces are about the size of peas.

To make the persimmon mixture: In a large bowl, combine the persimmons, raspberries, and sugar. Place in the prepared baking dish. Cut the butter into small pieces and sprinkle evenly over the fruit mixture.

Crumble the oat topping over the fruit. Bake for 40 minutes, or until the fruit is soft and the topping is lightly browned.

Makes 8 servings

Per serving: 487 calories, 6 g protein, 100 g carbohydrates, 12 g fat, 27 mg cholesterol, 15 g fiber, 11 mg sodium

The beauty and interest of this wonderful crisp is surpassed only by the delicate and aromatic qualities of persimmons. Only use Fuyu persimmons, the ones that are flat and shaped like tiny pumpkins. In general, this fruit comes from specialty orchards or private yards and is grown organically.

KITCHEN TIP

To keep this crisp in the spirit of this book, which means using organic fruits, keep the topping the same, but use whatever seasonal organic fruits are available. In spring, cherries and apricots are wonderful; in summer, use berries and peaches; and in the dark of winter, consider plumping up dried fruits along with apples for a hearty crisp.

APPLE-ASIAGO PIE

Crust

1½	cups whole grain pastry flour	½	cup very cold unsalted butter
1½	teaspoons dried thyme	½	cup milk
¼	teaspoon salt		

Topping

1	cup whole grain pastry flour	½	teaspoon freshly ground black pepper
1	cup packed brown sugar	6	tablespoons very cold unsalted butter
1	cup (2 ounces) grated Asiago cheese		

Filling

6	large crisp apples (such as Granny Smith), peeled, cored, and thinly sliced	1	tablespoon cornstarch
¾	cup packed brown sugar	¼	teaspoon freshly grated nutmeg

To make the crust: In a large bowl, combine the flour, thyme, and salt. Grate the butter into the mixture. Using your hands or a pastry blender, work the butter into the flour mixture until the pieces are about the size of peas. Add the milk, ¼ cup at a time, and blend until a soft, moist dough is formed. Add a few more tablespoons milk if the dough seems dry. It should be somewhat sticky.

Form the dough into a ball, then flatten into a round disk. Wrap in plastic wrap and refrigerate for at least 1 hour.

To make the topping: In a medium bowl, combine the flour, brown sugar, cheese, and pepper. Grate the butter into the mixture. Using your hands or a pastry blender, work the butter into the flour mixture until the pieces are about the size of peas. Refrigerate until ready to use.

Preheat the oven to 350°F. When the crust dough is chilled, place it on a well-floured surface and roll to about a ⅛" thickness, turning and flouring the dough often to keep it well-floured. Fold the dough in half and place in a 9" or 10" pie plate. Turn under and crimp the crust.

To make the filling: In a large bowl, combine the apples, brown sugar, cornstarch, and nutmeg. Place in the prepared crust. Crumble the crumb topping over the apples.

Bake for 1 hour, or until the crust is browned and the apples are soft. Place on a rack to cool for at least 30 minutes before slicing.

Makes 10 servings
Per serving: 446 calories, 8 g protein, 58 g carbohydrates, 21 g fat, 56 mg cholesterol, 3 g fiber, 266 mg sodium

SEEDS OF CHANGE™

In 1989, a group of eclectic individuals banded together around a common mission. Some were organic farmers, and others were seed collectors. One of these individuals was Alan Kapuler who, with a Ph.D. in molecular biology and a fertile mind, had left the groves of academia many years earlier for the Pacific Northwest and a new passion: organic gardening.

"As a gardener, you can fulfill a destiny: God is closer to you in the garden than anywhere else," says Kapuler. "We believe deeply in the ability to grow food in a different way so that you nourish the Earth while producing healthy, nutritious food."

The loss of diversity in food crops as well as all species of plants and animals was also at the forefront of his mind. It was a deeply rooted concern over these issues that led to the founding of Seeds of Change™. Started as a 100% Certified Organic seed company located in Santa Fe, New Mexico, the Seeds of Change mission is to preserve biodiversity and promote sustainable organic agricultural practices. Today, they also have a range of 100% Certified Organic foods including pasta sauces, salsas, rice and grain blends, salad dressings, and ketchup.

"We started with just our own farm, growing all our seeds ourselves. Even today, we grow more than 750 varieties a year, to trial, se-

Scott Vlaun

The Seeds of Change Research Farm at dawn, Santa Fe, New Mexico

lect, and breed new varieties as well as examine our existing varieties. But I'm happy to say that we also need our network of certified organic family farmers to whom, in many cases, we have taught the art of saving seed," says Stephen Badger, company president.

The company's own farm has yielded some wonderful results. When Rutgers University researchers tested the popular Peacevine Cherry Tomato (which Seeds of Change bred) against other varieties, they found that it contained the most vitamin C.

The expertise required to grow, clean, store, and pack seed is quite complicated. "Saving seeds is a tough endeavor," says Badger. "It takes a lot of knowledge as to when to harvest seed or even clean it properly, for that matter. But we believe deeply in preserving heirloom and traditional varieties for future generations, and we've essentially taught ourselves how to do it properly on a large scale."

Heirloom, traditional, and open pollinated varieties of seeds are typically not used in modern agriculture, and because of this, they are being lost for future generations. In many cases, seed varieties, if not used and saved, simply become extinct as they stop being passed from one generation to the next. This is a concern because once lost, those varieties may never again be available to help us cope with climate changes, soil changes, insects, and diseases.

So Seeds of Change offers to gardeners open pollinated varieties, which means that gardeners can save the seeds themselves. "It's certainly a bit of a self-defeating business proposition but every year we have new varieties, and we are committed to future generations having access to these varieties," says Badger. And all the varieties they offer are free of genetic modification.

"Walking through our fields is always a treat . . . a delight for the senses in terms of colors, scents, and tastes," states Badger. "We've always wanted to capture that freshness and goodness in a range of foods. In 1997, we started doing just that."

While regulations require that only 95% of ingredients in a food need to be organic to call it so, Seeds of Change believes in 100% Certified Organic, so you can trust that their foods and seeds are organic through and through.

"With our foods, we have a number of familiar favorites, but we also look to our seed heritage for guidance. So we mix everyday flavors like basil and other herbs with traditional grains like quinoa. An ancient grain from South America, quinoa has a nutty flavor, an extremely high protein content, and it provides a balanced source of amino acids," says Badger. "Or, we look to the pasilla pepper, a wonderful variety we came to through our interest in the diversity of peppers. It has a classic rich and smoky flavor."

Seeds of Change is also devoted to education and information. Visit their extensive Web site at www.seedsofchange.com.

Peacevine Cherry Tomato, a Seeds of Change original variety

Scott Vlaun

Inspecting a new kale variety for aphids at the research farm

Dave Smith

EARLY WINTER

My cooking is always at its best during the winter months. Even though I live in northern California, winters still bring back memories of days gone by, when I lived in a rural town in central Maine. The winters there were stubbornly long. The lake within view of my front yard sometimes didn't thaw until May. Summers quickly came and went.

With the days shorter during winter, I tend to spend more time at home, watching videos, folding laundry, or doing other homey activities while a pot of goodness simmers on my kitchen stove. I rely on more canned, dried, and frozen organic foods. I prepare a lot of savory slow-cooking dishes made with grains and pastas and use more spices and heartier herbs. Winter cooking can fill a house for hours with a medley of wonderful, soulful aromas that waft and dance from room to room. These scents warm me like a favorite throw blanket or thick wool sweater. Since

not a lot of fresh food is available, I honor anything that I can get my hands on. Winter foods may not be as bright and light as summer crops, but they provide soulful comfort.

Meals at this time of the year should be nurturing, hearty, and savored. During cold months, we naturally hunger for heartier dishes that fill our bellies with warmth and satisfaction and provide the energy we need.

KITCHEN TIP

Another way to prepare this free-form tart is by baking it on a pizza stone. Or, for a more formal tart, shape the dough in a tart pan.

PEAR, BRIE, AND OLIVE TART

Crust

1	cup unbleached all-purpose flour	½	teaspoon freshly ground black pepper
¼	cup very finely ground walnuts	½	cup unsalted butter
½	teaspoon salt	½	cup ice water

Filling

1	red onion, thinly sliced	4	ounces Brie cheese, cut into small pieces
2	pears, cored and thinly sliced	½	cup kalamata olives, pitted and halved
2	tablespoons sugar		
2	teaspoons chopped fresh thyme		

To make the crust: In a large bowl, combine the flour, walnuts, salt, and pepper. Grate the butter into the mixture. Using your hands or a pastry blender, work the butter into the flour mixture until the pieces are about the size of peas.

Add the water, 1 tablespoon at a time, and blend until a soft, moist dough is formed. Form the dough into a ball, then flatten into a round disk. Wrap in plastic wrap and refrigerate for at least 1 hour.

Preheat oven to 400°F. Line a baking sheet with parchment paper

On a well-floured board, roll the dough into a ⅛" thick oval. Fold the dough in half and place in the center of the prepared baking sheet. The edges will fall over the side.

To make the filling: Arrange the onion in the center of the crust, leaving a 1½" to 2" edge to roll as a hand-formed crust. Arrange the pears on top and sprinkle with the sugar and thyme. Top with the Brie and olives. Using your hands, roll the outer part of the dough under to form a crust. Crimp the edges.

Bake for 20 to 30 minutes, or until the crust is golden brown.

Makes 8 servings

Per serving: 318 calories, 7 g protein, 27 g carbohydrates, 21 g fat, 47 mg cholesterol, 3 g fiber, 311 mg sodium

This is one of my favorite salads. Its origin comes from my grandfather, who used to pick wild dandelions from our neighbors' yards. Using a bold, fruity olive oil and good quality red wine vinegar is one of the keys to the success of this robust salad.

KITCHEN TIP

This is one salad that is actually good the next day. I like it tucked into sandwiches, with salty meats or pungent cheeses.

BITTER GREEN AND EGG SALAD

¼ cup extra virgin olive oil

3 tablespoons red wine vinegar

1 tablespoon brown sugar

1–2 garlic cloves, thinly sliced

¼ teaspoon salt

¼ teaspoon freshly ground black pepper

2 heads bitter greens (such as frisée, radicchio, endive, and dandelion), torn into bite-size pieces

2 green onions, thinly sliced

3 hard-cooked eggs, peeled and chopped

1 tablespoon capers

In a large bowl, whisk together the oil, vinegar, sugar, garlic, salt, and pepper. Add the greens and green onions and toss to coat well.

Top with the eggs and capers.

Makes 6 servings
Per serving: 144 calories, 4 g protein, 6 g carbohydrates, 12 g fat, 106 mg cholesterol, 1 g fiber, 114 mg sodium

DEVILED CRAB DIP

2	large eggs	2	tablespoons chopped fresh Italian parsley
1½	tablespoons butter		
2	tablespoons grated red onion	2	teaspoons Dijon mustard
1½	tablespoons unbleached all-purpose flour	½	teaspoon salt
			Pinch of ground red pepper
1	cup milk	4	cups lump crabmeat

Preheat the oven to 375°F. Lightly butter a 2-quart baking dish.

In a small bowl, beat the eggs; set aside.

In a medium saucepan over medium heat, melt the butter. Add the onion and cook for 1 minute. Add the flour and cook, stirring constantly, for 2 minutes, or until the mixture bubbles. Gradually whisk in the milk. Cook, stirring frequently, for 5 minutes, or until the mixture forms a thick sauce.

Remove from the heat. Add about one-quarter of the hot mixture to the bowl with the eggs, stirring quickly. Add the egg mixture back into the sauce, stirring quickly. Stir in the parsley, mustard, salt, and pepper.

Gently stir in the crabmeat.

Place in the prepared baking dish and bake for 40 minutes, or until the top browns and a knife inserted in the center comes out clean.

Makes 6 servings

Per serving: 245 calories, 39 g protein, 4 g carbohydrates, 8 g fat, 202 mg cholesterol, 0 g fiber, 853 mg sodium

This recipe is an adaptation of my mom's recipe that remains a favorite in my memories from childhood.

KITCHEN TIP

For a lovely lunch or light supper, bake the deviled crab in individual baking dishes. When baked, allow to stand for 5 minutes, then invert on individual plates with salad and garlic toast.

You can use any cut of chicken for this dish, but my preference is to roast a whole chicken. I like serving it family style, with the whole roast chicken perched on top of the mashed vegetables. Round out the meal with steamed vegetables such as broccoli or Brussels sprouts.

ROAST CHICKEN WITH MASHED VEGETABLES

1	teaspoon cumin	1	large onion, thinly sliced
1	teaspoon paprika	1	pound potatoes, peeled and cut into wedges
½	teaspoon salt	1	pound turnips, peeled and cut into wedges
½	teaspoon freshly ground black pepper	¼	cup chicken broth or milk
1	roasting chicken (3 to 4 pounds)	2	tablespoons chopped fresh parsley
2	tablespoons olive oil		

Preheat the oven to 475°F.

In a small bowl, combine the cumin, paprika, salt, and pepper. Place the chicken on a rack in a large roasting pan. Rub half of the cumin mixture over the chicken and season the inside of the chicken with the remaining cumin mixture. Roast for 20 minutes. Reduce the heat to 375°F and continue roasting for 1 to 1¼ hours, or until a thermometer inserted in a breast registers 180°F and the juices run clear. Let stand for 10 minutes before carving.

Meanwhile, heat the oil in a medium skillet over medium heat. Add the onion, cover, and cook for 6 minutes, or until very soft.

Bring a large pot of salted water to a boil. Add the potatoes and turnips and cook for 15 minutes, or until tender. Drain and place in a large bowl. Mash the potatoes and turnips, adding the broth or milk until creamy. Stir in the onion and season with salt and pepper.

Spoon all the mashed vegetables onto a large serving platter. Remove the chicken from the oven and place on the vegetables.

Skim the pan juices and pour over the chicken and vegetables. Sprinkle with the parsley.

Makes 6 servings

Per serving: 460 calories, 54 g protein, 19 g carbohydrates, 19 g fat, 198 mg cholesterol, 3 g fiber, 546 mg sodium

CURRIED CHICKEN SALAD

1   cup low-fat plain yogurt

2   tablespoons honey

1½ teaspoons curry powder

2   cooked boneless, skinless
    chicken breast halves, cut
    into bite-size pieces

1   apple, peeled and
    chopped

2   small celery ribs, thinly
    sliced

1   green onion, thinly sliced

½   cup walnuts, toasted

    Salt

    Freshly ground black
    pepper

1   head Boston lettuce

In a large bowl, combine the yogurt, honey, and curry powder. Add
the chicken, apple, celery, green onion, and walnuts. Toss to coat
well and season with salt and pepper to taste.

Line 4 plates with the lettuce leaves. Top with scoops of the salad.

Makes 4 servings

*Per serving: 265 calories, 20 g protein, 26 g carbohydrates, 10 g fat, 37 mg cholesterol,
4 g fiber, 112 mg sodium*

*I have to keep myself from
devouring this chicken salad
while preparing it, taking just
a few too many tastes. I like to
serve it as a salad, but it is just
as delicious on thick slices of
whole grain bread or whole
wheat pitas.*

KITCHEN TIP

For a wonderful vegetarian
salad, substitute seasoned
firm tofu for the chicken.

This aromatic dish is even better when served the next day. It is similar to a recipe from my childhood, Tsimmis, which my mom made at Rosh Hashanah, the Jewish New Year. The combination of the yams and dried fruit symbolizes a wish for sweetness in the new year, which somehow made this dish taste even better to me.

GAME HEN WITH AROMATIC SWEET POTATOES AND PRUNES

1½	pounds sweet potatoes, peeled and cubed	4	small game hens
1	large onion, thinly sliced	2	cups boiling chicken broth
2	tablespoons olive oil	3	tablespoons brown sugar
1	teaspoon turmeric	2	teaspoons ground cinnamon
1	teaspoon paprika	1½	cups pitted prunes
1	teaspoon ground coriander	½	cup canned chickpeas, rinsed and drained
¼	teaspoon salt	¼	cup chopped fresh cilantro
¼	teaspoon freshly ground black pepper		Pinch of saffron (optional)

Preheat the oven to 400°F.

In a large, deep roasting pan, toss the sweet potatoes and onion with 1 tablespoon of the oil.

In a small bowl, combine the turmeric, paprika, coriander, salt, and pepper.

Rub the hens with the remaining 1 tablespoon oil and generously sprinkle with the spice mixture.

Place the hens on the sweet potatoes and roast for 30 minutes.

In a medium saucepan, combine the broth, brown sugar, cinnamon, prunes, chickpeas, cilantro, and saffron, if using. Bring to a boil over high heat.

Remove the baking dish from the oven and pour the prune mixture over the potatoes, stirring to blend. Reduce the heat to 350°F. Bake, stirring the potatoes occasionally, for 45 to 55 minutes, or until a thermometer inserted in a breast registers 170°F and the juices run clear. Let stand for 10 minutes before serving.

Makes 4 servings
Per serving: 757 calories, 59 g protein, 100 g carbohydrates, 15 g fat, 233 mg cholesterol, 13 g fiber, 816 mg sodium

Cornmeal-Crusted Cod with Garlicky Spinach and Honey-Glazed Carrots (page 223)

CORNMEAL-CRUSTED COD WITH GARLICKY SPINACH

4	cod or scrod fillets (about 4 ounces each)	¼–1	teaspoon ground red pepper
1½	cups buttermilk	4	tablespoons olive oil
1	cup cornmeal	2	garlic cloves, minced
3	tablespoons chopped fresh parsley	2	pounds fresh spinach, steamed
1	tablespoon dried oregano		Juice of 1 large lemon
2	teaspoons dried thyme	1	tablespoon soy sauce
1½	teaspoons salt		Zest of 1 lemon
½	teaspoon freshly ground black pepper		

The night before serving, place the fillets in a bowl and pour the buttermilk over all. Toss to coat. Cover and refrigerate.

Preheat the oven to 250°F.

In a pie plate, combine the cornmeal, parsley, oregano, thyme, salt, black pepper, and red pepper. Remove the fish from the buttermilk, shaking off any excess. Dip the fish in the cornmeal mixture, turning to coat completely.

Heat 1½ tablespoons of the oil in a large skillet over medium heat. Add 2 fillets and cook for 8 to 10 minutes, turning once, or until browned and the fish flakes easily. Place on a baking sheet and keep warm in the oven. Repeat with 1½ tablespoons of the remaining oil and 2 fillets.

Wipe the skillet clean and heat the remaining 1 tablespoon oil over medium heat. Add the garlic and cook for 2 minutes. Add the spinach, lemon juice, and soy sauce and cook for 3 minutes, or until heated through. Place on a serving platter and top with the fillets. Sprinkle with the lemon zest.

Makes 4 servings

Per serving: 407 calories, 33 g protein, 33 g carbohydrates, 17 g fat, 52 mg cholesterol, 24 g fiber, 989 mg sodium

The combination of cod, cornmeal, and spinach in this recipe is wonderful. A few drops of hot sauce can really pull it all together. Allow about one bunch of fresh spinach per person.

KITCHEN TIP

Frozen spinach works well in this recipe. Simply thaw and squeeze it dry, then add to the skillet with the garlic and cook until heated through.

Rich, tender seafood marries beautifully with thin strands of pasta, tender chard, and a creamy tomato sauce.

KITCHEN TIP

If you don't want to bother with lobster, substitute ¾ pound shrimp or scallops.

SEAFOOD ANGEL HAIR PASTA

1	lobster tail (about 1 pound)	2	teaspoons lime zest
2	tablespoons butter	1	cup heavy cream (optional)
2	tablespoons olive oil	12	ounces angel hair pasta
4–6	garlic cloves, minced	1	pound fresh chard, chopped coarsely
2	shallots, thinly sliced	1	pound clams (such as littleneck, manilla, or cherrystone), scrubbed
1	can (14½ ounces) diced tomatoes		Salt
1	cup clam juice or chicken broth		Freshly ground black pepper
½	cup dry vermouth		Pinch of ground red or chipotle pepper (optional)
1	tablespoon chopped fresh thyme		
1	teaspoon paprika		

Cut down the belly side of the lobster tail and remove the meat. Remove all fibrous or dark-colored membranes and cut the meat into bite-size pieces. Refrigerate until ready to use.

Cut the lobster shell into 4 pieces.

Heat the butter and oil in a large saucepan over medium-high heat. Add the garlic and shallots and cook for 2 minutes. Add the tomatoes (with juice), clam juice or broth, vermouth, and lobster shells. Bring to a boil. Reduce the heat to low, cover, and simmer for 15 minutes.

Remove and discard the lobster shells. Add the thyme, paprika, lime zest, and cream, if using. Cook, uncovered, for 20 minutes, or until reduced by a one-third.

Add the lobster meat and clams. Season to taste with the salt, black pepper, and red or chipotle pepper. Cover and simmer for 3 to 5 minutes, or until the clams open and the lobster turns opaque. Discard any unopened clams.

Meanwhile, cook the pasta according to package directions, adding the chard during the last 1 minute of cooking time. Drain and place in a large bowl. Pour the seafood sauce over the pasta.

Makes 6 servings

Per serving: 466 calories, 34 g protein, 49 g carbohydrates, 13 g fat, 161 mg cholesterol, 4 g fiber, 1,434 mg sodium

SWEET-AND-SOUR CABBAGE WITH SMOKED PORK CHOPS

1   tablespoon olive oil

1   head cabbage, cored and very thinly sliced

1   red onion, thinly sliced

½   cup packed brown sugar

½   cup rice wine vinegar

    Salt

    Freshly ground black pepper

4   smoked pork chops (about 5 ounces each)

4   tablespoons Dijon mustard

1   tablespoon honey

This dish is one of my all-time favorites. Slow-cooking cabbage and onion brings out a mellow, soft flavor that is further enhanced by a touch of brown sugar and vinegar. It is wonderful with smoked meats.

Heat the oil in a Dutch oven over medium heat. Add the cabbage and onion and cook, stirring, for 2 minutes. Reduce the heat to low, cover, and cook, stirring often, for 45 minutes, or until very soft.

Add the brown sugar and vinegar and cook for 5 minutes longer. Season with salt and pepper to taste.

Place the chops on top of the cabbage. Cover and cook for 20 minutes, or until the chops are heated through.

Meanwhile, in a small bowl, combine the mustard and honey.

Remove the cabbage mixture to a large platter and top with the chops. Drizzle the mustard mixture over the chops.

Makes 4 servings

Per serving: 310 calories, 21 g protein, 36 g carbohydrates, 10 g fat, 45 mg cholesterol, 2 g fiber, 1,666 mg sodium

POT ROAST WITH WINTER VEGETABLES

1	chuck or bottom round roast (about 3 pounds)	2	tablespoons chopped fresh thyme
½	teaspoon salt	3	large sweet potatoes, peeled and cut into large chunks
¼	teaspoon freshly ground black pepper		
4	cups vegetable or beef broth	3	large leeks, whites only, sliced and washed thoroughly
2	tablespoons Dijon mustard	12	dried apricot halves, chopped
10	large garlic cloves, chopped		

Preheat the oven to 500°F.

Place the roast in a large roasting pan and sprinkle with the salt and pepper. Roast for 45 minutes, turning once.

Meanwhile, in a large measuring cup, combine the broth, mustard, garlic, and thyme.

Reduce the heat to 350°F. Pour the broth mixture over the meat, cover, and roast for 1 hour. Add the sweet potatoes, leeks, and apricots.

Roast for 2 hours, or until the meat is very tender when tested with a fork.

Makes 8 servings

Per serving: 459 calories, 61 g protein, 23 g carbohydrates, 14 g fat, 171 mg cholesterol, 4 g fiber, 629 mg sodium

Having gone through lean financial times, I learned how to cook with cuts of meat that are less expensive and typically need slow cooking to tenderize the meat. Chuck or pot roast is a cut of beef that I love. Through hours of cooking over low heat, the meat becomes tender, absorbing seasonings and flavors of the ingredients that are cooked alongside.

ROASTED RUTABAGA
WITH SAUSAGE

When oven-roasted, rutabagas turn golden and creamy. This dish reminds me of food that one might find in a country pub in the north of England. If you can't find lamb sausage, pork or chicken will work just as well.

2 pounds lamb sausage

1 large rutabaga (about ¾ pound), peeled and cut into thick wedges

1 large red onion, sliced

3–4 garlic cloves, minced

1 tablespoon chopped fresh rosemary

½ cup blackberry or raspberry preserves

2–3 tablespoons balsamic vinegar

Salt

Freshly ground black pepper

Preheat the oven to 500°F. Place the sausage in a large shallow roasting pan. Cook, turning occasionally, for 15 minutes, or until no longer pink.

Reduce the temperature to 350°F. Remove the sausage to a plate and add the rutabaga, onion, garlic, rosemary, and preserves to the pan with the sausage drippings. Toss to coat well. Place the sausage on top of the vegetables. Cover and roast, tossing occasionally, for 45 minutes, or until the vegetables are tender and the sausage is cooked through.

Transfer the sausage to a platter. Drizzle the vinegar over the vegetables. Mix well and season with salt and pepper to taste. Serve with the sausage.

Makes 6 servings

Per serving: 431 calories, 20 g protein, 27 g carbohydrates, 27 g fat, 83 mg cholesterol, 3 g fiber, 93 mg sodium

SPANISH TORTILLA

6	tablespoons extra virgin olive oil	6	eggs, beaten
2	large parsnips, thinly sliced	3	tablespoons chopped fresh parsley
1	onion, thinly sliced	½	teaspoon salt
2	large red potatoes, thickly sliced	¼	teaspoon freshly ground black pepper

Heat 1 tablespoon of the oil in a large nonstick omelette pan or skillet over medium heat. Add the parsnips and onion and cook, turning often, for 10 minutes, or until browned and tender. Remove to a large bowl.

Add 1 tablespoon of the remaining oil to the skillet, then add the potatoes. Cook, turning often, for 15 minutes, or until browned and tender. Remove to the bowl with the parsnips.

Add the eggs, parsley, salt, and pepper to the bowl. Toss to mix well.

Wipe the skillet and add 2 tablespoons of the remaining oil. Pour the egg mixture into the pan. Place the pan over medium heat and cook, covered, for 15 minutes, or until the eggs start to set and the bottom browns.

Place a plate on top of the pan and invert the tortilla onto the plate. Add the remaining 2 tablespoons oil to the pan and slide the tortilla back into the pan. Cook for 5 minutes longer, or until browned. Slide onto a plate. Allow to cool to room temperature and cut into wedges to serve.

Makes 8 servings

Per serving: 201 calories, 6 g protein, 14 g carbohydrates, 14 g fat, 159 mg cholesterol, 2 g fiber, 197 mg sodium

A tortilla, which is similar to a giant inverted omelette, is eaten as snack food throughout Spain. Available at all times of the day, I especially enjoyed it while sipping sherry or Cava (Spanish sparkling wine) in small neighborhood bars. Traditionally, it is made with only potatoes. I use parsnips as well to add a creamy and sweet quality to this classic dish.

KITCHEN TIP

To make gnocchi light and fluffy, use as little flour as possible. You do need enough to make them hold together, but too much makes them heavy. By testing one at the beginning, when you first roll them, you can tell if more flour is needed.

GNOCCHI WITH SAGE BUTTER

Gnocchi

2	large russet potatoes (about 1½ pounds)		1	teaspoon salt
1	large egg, beaten		½–1	cup unbleached all-purpose flour

Sauce

3	tablespoons butter		¼	cup dry vermouth
1	shallot, minced			Salt
1	garlic clove, minced			Freshly ground black pepper
3	tablespoons chopped fresh sage		¼	cup (1 ounce) grated Romano cheese
¼	cup minced fresh parsley			

To make the gnocchi: Preheat the oven to 450°F.

Pierce the potatoes and bake for 50 to 65 minutes, or until very soft. Remove and set aside until cool enough to handle.

Bring a large pot of water to boil over high heat. Cut the potatoes in half, scoop out the flesh, and discard the skins. Push the flesh through a potato ricer or mash thoroughly with a fork and place in a large bowl. Stir in the egg and salt.

Add the flour, ¼ cup at a time, using your hands and blending just until the dough holds together. Remove 1 teaspoon of the dough and roll into a ball on a floured surface. Drop into the boiling water. If the piece falls apart, add more flour to the dough, 2 tablespoons at a time, until the dough forms a ball. Repeat the cooking test until the gnocchi holds together and floats to the surface.

Turn the dough out onto a well-floured board. Divide the dough into 5 pieces and roll each into a ¾"-thick rope, being sure to roll the ropes in flour to keep from sticking. Cut each rope into ¾" pieces. Roll each piece with a floured fork or thumb and make a slight indention. Dust the gnocchi with flour. If not cooking right away, place on a baking pan, cover, and refrigerate or freeze until ready to cook.

To cook the gnocchi, add salt to the boiling water and drop the gnocchi into the water. Cook until they rise to the surface. Remove with a slotted spoon to a colander.

To make the sauce: Melt the butter in a medium saucepan over medium heat. Add the shallot, garlic, and sage and cook for 4 minutes, or until lightly browned. Add the parsley and vermouth. Season with salt and pepper to taste. Place the gnocchi in a serving bowl and top with the sauce and cheese.

Makes 4 servings

Per serving: 306 calories, 9 g protein, 50 g carbohydrates, 6 g fat, 65 mg cholesterol, 2 g fiber, 730 mg sodium

HONEY-GLAZED CARROTS

1	tablespoon butter	¼	cup honey
1	leek, white part only, halved, sliced, and washed thoroughly	1	cinnamon stick
		1	teaspoon ground cumin
1	pound carrots, sliced	2	teaspoons chopped fresh mint
1	cup apple juice	¼	teaspoon salt

Melt the butter in a medium saucepan over medium-high heat. Add the leek and cook for 2 minutes, or until lightly browned. Add the carrots and cook for 2 minutes, or until lightly browned.

Add the apple juice, honey, cinnamon stick, cumin, mint, and salt and bring to a boil. Reduce the heat to low, cover, and simmer for 15 minutes, or until the carrots are very soft. Remove and discard the cinnamon stick before serving.

Makes 6 servings

Per serving: 128 calories, 1 g protein, 27 g carbohydrates, 3 g fat, 5 mg cholesterol, 3 g fiber, 151 mg sodium

The aroma and flavor of these carrots are enticing. I like them with roasted lamb, served along with saffron-scented rice or couscous.

(photograph on page 214)

KITCHEN TIP

This honey sauce is terrific with frozen vegetables, too. Replace the carrots with a bag of frozen peas and carrots, but add the frozen vegetables after cooking the sauce for 10 minutes.

Gnocchi with Sage Butter

CHARD AND FETA PIE

2 cups shredded potatoes (about 2 large)

2 green onions, minced

¾ teaspoon salt

6 eggs

¼ cup unbleached all-purpose flour

¼ teaspoon freshly ground black pepper

2 tablespoons olive oil

1 red onion, finely chopped

2 garlic cloves, minced

2 bunches green or red chard or spinach, coarsely chopped

1½ cups (8 ounces) crumbled feta cheese

1 cup milk

2 tablespoons chopped fresh oregano

½ cup toasted bread crumbs

Preheat the oven to 400°F. Lightly oil a 9" deep-dish pie plate.

Place the potatoes and green onions in a colander and sprinkle with ½ teaspoon of the salt. Drain for 5 minutes, gently squeezing out any excess liquid.

Place in a medium bowl and add 1 of the eggs, the flour, and pepper. Stir until well-blended. Press into the prepared pie plate to form a crust. Brush with 1 tablespoon of the oil. Bake for 30 minutes, or until the crust is browned.

Meanwhile, heat the remaining 1 tablespoon oil in a medium skillet over medium-high heat. Add the red onion and cook for 4 minutes, or until soft. Add the garlic and chard or spinach and cook, stirring often, for 3 minutes, or until the chard or spinach is wilted. Remove from the heat, drain off excess liquid, and cool slightly.

In a large bowl, combine the remaining 5 eggs, 1 cup of the cheese, the milk, oregano, the remaining ¼ teaspoon salt, and the chard mixture. Pour into the baked crust. Sprinkle the top with the bread crumbs and the remaining ½ cup cheese.

Reduce the heat to 350°F. Bake for 35 minutes, or until a knife inserted in the center comes out clean. Let stand for 15 minutes before cutting.

Makes 8 servings

Per serving: 318 calories, 14 g protein, 32 g carbohydrates, 15 g fat, 215 mg cholesterol, 2 g fiber, 685 mg sodium

Stan Frankenthaler

Salamander Restaurant, Cambridge, Massachusetts

Courtesy of Salamander Restaurant

As food professionals, we take the responsibility of making food choices for our customers—we roast our own meats, bake our own breads, and make our own condiments. Our goal is to make sure that the food we serve is flavorful and good for you.

CORN AND SWEET POTATO STEW

2	tablespoons toasted sesame oil
1	onion, minced
1	tablespoon minced ginger
1	tablespoon minced garlic
1	teaspoon kosher salt
2	teaspoons ground black pepper
3	cups vegetable stock or water
1	cup white wine
½	cup mirin
½	cup rice vinegar
2	cups coconut milk

1¼	pounds sweet potatoes, peeled and diced
8	ears fresh corn, shucked, roasted, kernels cut from cob
1	tablespoon chili paste
1	tablespoon coriander seed, toasted and cracked
2	tablespoons green curry paste (fresh or canned)
2	tablespoons coarsely chopped mint leaves
2	tablespoons coarsely chopped cilantro leaves
2	tablespoons lime juice

In a large saucepan, heat the sesame oil over medium-high heat. Sauté the onion, ginger, and garlic until lightly browned. Season with salt and pepper. Add all liquids, sweet potatoes, corn, chili paste, and coriander and bring to a boil; reduce the heat to a simmer and cook until sweet potatoes are tender.

Remove from the heat. Just prior to serving, stir in the curry paste, fresh herbs, and lime juice. Adjust seasoning, if necessary.

Makes 8 servings

FARMER STU'S KALE SALAD

1 large bunch kale, thinly
   sliced

¼ cup extra virgin olive oil

1 small red onion, thinly
   sliced

2 garlic cloves, minced

3 tablespoons balsamic
   vinegar

1 hot chile pepper (such as
   jalapeño, serrano, or
   habenaro), seeded and
   minced

Salt

Freshly ground black
pepper

Place the kale in a large serving bowl; set aside at room temperature.

Heat the oil in a small saucepan over medium-low heat. Add the onion and garlic and cook for 6 minutes, or until very soft. Add the vinegar and chile pepper. Cook for 1 minute. Pour the mixture over the kale and toss well. Season with salt and black pepper to taste. Serve immediately.

Makes 4 servings

Per serving: 191 calories, 3 g protein, 15 g carbohydrates, 14 g fat, 0 mg cholesterol, 2 g fiber, 40 mg sodium

Stuart Dickson, who owns the farm that grows most of the food for my restaurants, is a fantastic cook, and he takes great pride in his use of greens. He especially loves kale, and sometimes instead of kale, he uses baby escarole leaves, which are equally delicious with this hot dressing.

KITCHEN TIP

I love this salad with bits of soft goat cheese crumbled over the top.

ORANGE BEETS AND OLIVES

6 beets, trimmed and
   scrubbed

2 blood oranges, halved

½ cup kalamata olives, pitted

3 tablespoons balsamic
   vinegar

2 tablespoons extra virgin
   olive oil

2 tablespoons grated fresh
   ginger

2 tablespoons chopped
   fresh chives

Salt

Place the beets in a medium saucepan and cover with water. Bring to a boil over high heat. Reduce the heat to low, cover, and simmer for 45 minutes, or until the beets are tender.

Drain the beets and run under cold water to remove the skins. Cut the beets into ¼" cubes and place in a large bowl.

Squeeze the juice from the oranges over the beets. Add the olives, vinegar, oil, ginger, and chives. Toss to coat well and let sit for 5 minutes. Season with salt to taste.

Makes 4 servings

Per serving: 176 calories, 3 g protein, 23 g carbohydrates, 9 g fat, 0 mg cholesterol, 5 g fiber, 248 mg sodium

The combination of sweet beets and tangy oranges is taken to a higher palate pleasure with the salty olives and zesty chives.

KITCHEN TIP

If you can't find blood oranges, use ½ cup orange juice instead.

You either love fruitcake or you don't. I find that it is the candied fruit that turns people away. In this recipe, dried organic fruit is used instead of the sugary, artificial colored fruit. In combination with the ginger cake, this cake is one that celebrates the holiday season and is almost too good to call fruitcake.

KITCHEN TIPS

This cake screams for ice cream. At this time of the year, you might find pumpkin ice cream, which would be wonderful. Otherwise, go with pure vanilla or honey-vanilla.

Make individual fruitcakes using cupcake tins and serve with homemade warm custard for a spectacular holiday treat.

GINGERBREAD FRUITCAKE

1⅓	cups unbleached all-purpose flour	½	cup packed brown sugar or honey
1	teaspoon baking powder	½	cup molasses
1	teaspoon ground cinnamon	1	large egg, beaten
1	teaspoon ground ginger	¾	cup buttermilk
¾	teaspoon freshly ground black pepper	1	teaspoon vanilla extract
¾	teaspoon allspice	1½	cups dried fruit, finely chopped (such as apricots, cherries, cranberries, figs, dates, and apples)
½	teaspoon baking soda		
½	teaspoon salt	½	cup chopped walnuts or pecans
⅓	cup butter, softened		

Preheat the oven to 375°F. Lightly butter a 10" springform pan.

In a medium bowl, combine the flour, baking powder, cinnamon, ginger, pepper, allspice, baking soda, and salt.

In another medium bowl, with an electric mixer on medium speed, beat the butter and brown sugar or honey until creamy. Beat in the molasses, egg, buttermilk, and vanilla extract.

On low speed, gradually beat in the flour mixture just until blended. Stir in the dried fruit and nuts.

Pour into the prepared pan and bake for 35 minutes, or until a wooden pick inserted in the center comes out clean. Cool on a rack for 30 minutes. Remove from the pan and serve warm, or cool completely.

Makes 12 servings

Per serving: 349 calories, 5 g protein, 46 g carbohydrates, 17 g fat, 49 mg cholesterol, 2 g fiber, 332 mg sodium

DEEP OF WINTER

The heart of winter finds me in the kitchen wearing oversized sweat-shirts, baggy pants, and wool socks as I happily hum in front of my workhorse of a commercial gas stove. Strange as it sounds, this is my most favorite time of the year to cook. It seems easier to plan when you have limited choices. I savor the challenge of working with a smaller variety of fresh foods and finding ways to prepare meals that keep warmth, comfort, and heartiness simmering on the front burner.

But reality is reality. Attempting to prepare Mediterranean foods during the deep of winter can be an undertaking. I remember a very cold, very stormy February in which the farmers couldn't even get into their fields to

harvest. The chef at my restaurant looked up at me and declared, "Jesse, there is simply nothing growing, and most of the produce kept in storage is downright gone." Somehow, we managed to produce wonderful braised, stewed, and roasted dishes that kept our customers' bellies full, warm, and happy.

Anyone can prepare for winter, even those who live in the coldest of climates. Think of the deep of winter as payoff time. I do. The Indian Summer nights that I spent stacking fresh produce in my two food dryers are now reaping me rewards. Dried organic mushrooms, berries, figs, and tomatoes captured during their prime are ready for hearty dishes.

Enjoy these days. Spring is on its way.

Recipes

This classic warm anchovy dip appeared often as an appetizer at my Italian grandfather's house. The sweetness of broccoli, turnips, beets, cauliflower, or carrots is wonderful with the salty sauce.

KITCHEN TIP

Baugna cauda is best served warm. I like to serve it in a butter warmer or a cast-iron skillet on a warming tray. Don't worry if there are leftovers; just store it in the refrigerator for up to a week, using small amounts to season vegetables or as a sauce over grilled fish.

WINTER VEGETABLES WITH BAUGNA CAUDA

⅓ cup olive oil

¼ cup butter

3 cans (2 ounces each) anchovies packed in oil, drained

2 garlic cloves, thinly sliced

1½ teaspoons lemon zest

Pinch of crushed red-pepper flakes (optional)

5 cups vegetables (such as broccoli, turnips, beets, cauliflower, and carrots) cut into bite-size pieces

1 fennel bulb or 4 celery ribs, cut into 3" strips

In a medium saucepan over medium-high heat, bring the oil, butter, anchovies, garlic, and lemon zest to a boil. Reduce the heat to low and simmer for 5 minutes, or until the anchovies dissolve. Add the red-pepper flakes, if using. Place in a serving bowl.

Meanwhile, place 1" of water in a large saucepan over high heat. Bring to a boil and add a steamer basket or wire rack. Add the vegetables, reduce the heat to low, cover, and simmer for 8 minutes, or until the vegetables are tender-crisp. Remove and cool slightly. Place on a large serving platter with the fennel or celery. Serve with the sauce.

Makes 12 servings
Per serving: 131 calories, 4 g protein, 5 g carbohydrates, 11 g fat, 19 mg cholesterol, 2 g fiber, 417 mg sodium

TUSCAN-STYLE GRILLED BRUSCHETTA

2	tablespoons olive oil	½	red onion, minced
2	garlic cloves, minced	1	cup cooked white beans
4	cups mustard greens	2	teaspoons chopped fresh oregano
1	tablespoon balsamic vinegar	½	cup vegetable or chicken broth
	Salt	6	slices (½" each) Italian bread, toasted
	Freshly ground black pepper		

Heat 1 tablespoon of the oil in a medium skillet over medium-low heat. Add the garlic and greens and cook for 5 minutes, or until the greens are very tender. Stir in the vinegar. Remove to a bowl and set aside to cool slightly. Season generously with salt and pepper to taste.

Heat the remaining 1 tablespoon oil in the same skillet over medium heat. Add the onion and cook for 5 minutes, or until soft. Add the beans, oregano, and broth. Cook for 5 minutes, or until heated through and well-blended. Using a fork, coarsely mash the beans. Season with salt and pepper to taste.

Evenly divide the greens among the bread slices. Top each with an even portion of the bean mixture. Serve immediately.

Makes 6 servings

Per serving: 248 calories, 9 g protein, 40 g carbohydrates, 6 g fat, 0 mg cholesterol, 5 g fiber, 219 mg sodium

This combination of white beans, garlic, and spicy mustard greens is not only full of calcium but also jam-packed with flavor. There is nothing that compares with the creaminess of cooked dried white beans, but rinsed and drained canned beans work well in a pinch.

PARSNIP AND BEET SOUP WITH DILL CREAM

6 cups vegetable or chicken broth

1 pound parsnips, cut into small cubes

6 beets, trimmed and scrubbed

1 large shallot, thinly sliced

3 whole cloves

3 whole peppercorns

3 tablespoons sugar

Salt

Freshly ground black pepper

1 cup sour cream

1 green onion, finely chopped

2 tablespoons chopped fresh dill

Bring the broth to a boil in a large saucepan over high heat. Add the parsnips. Reduce the heat to low, cover, and simmer for 10 minutes, or until tender. Using a slotted spoon, remove the parsnips to a bowl.

Add the beets, shallot, cloves, and peppercorns to the simmering broth. Cover and simmer for 45 minutes, or until the beets are tender. Using a slotted spoon, remove the beets to the cutting board, reserving the liquid. When the beets are cool, slip off the skins. Cut into small cubes.

Strain the broth through a cheesecloth-lined sieve into a large bowl. Return the broth to the pot. Add the parsnips, beets, and sugar. Season to taste with salt and black pepper.

In a small bowl, combine the sour cream, green onion, and dill.

Ladle the soup into 6 bowls and top with the sour cream mixture.

Makes 6 servings

Per serving: 161 calories, 7 g protein, 23 g carbohydrates, 7 g fat, 14 mg cholesterol, 4 g fiber, 704 mg sodium

Parsnip and Beet Soup with Dill Cream and Rosemary-Lemon Biscuits (page 254)

Peter Hoffman

Savoy, New York City

Courtesy of the Savoy

At a time when consumption is so often associated with nonrenewable resources, our consumption and, hopefully, our conspicuous consumption of organic food is the best way that we can ensure the preservation of farmland and the continuity of good farm practices. Few acts of personal pleasure offer the possibility of such profound economic and social impact.

DUCK LEGS

2	tablespoons butter	1	tablespoon peppercorns
4	carrots, minced	4	cups chicken stock
1	large onion, minced	12	duck legs
1	bulb garlic, minced		Salt and pepper
3	cups red wine	8	cups water
3	bay leaves	2	tablespoons olive oil
2	sprigs fresh rosemary	1	clove garlic, minced
1	tablespoon allspice	6	cups escarole

Preheat the oven to 375°F.

Heat the butter in a large saucepan over high heat. Add the mirepoix (minced carrots, onion, and garlic) and brown, stirring frequently, for about 5 minutes. Add the wine to deglaze the pan. Over high heat, bring to a boil; add the bay leaves, rosemary, allspice, and peppercorns. Reduce the heat to medium-low and simmer for 5 minutes. Add the chicken stock and simmer for 5 minutes longer.

Pour the mixture into a large roasting pan. Place the duck legs on the mixture, adding water if necessary to cover the sides of the legs. (Do not let the top skin get covered by the liquid.) Season the legs with salt and pepper. Place in the oven and cook, uncov-

ered, for 1½ hours, or until the top skin is browned and lightly crisp. Remove the legs to a serving plate; strain and skim the stock.

Place the stock in a medium saucepan and bring to a boil over medium-high heat. Cook for 15 minutes, or until reduced by half.

Meanwhile, heat the olive oil in a large skillet. Add the garlic and cook for 3 minutes, or until golden. Add the escarole and cook, stirring, for 2 minutes. Add ¼ to ½ cup of the duck stock and stir until heated through. Season with salt and pepper.

To serve, place the duck legs on a plate and top with some of the reduced stock. Serve the escarole alongside.

Makes 6 servings

CHICKEN-VEGETABLE SOUP WITH NOODLES

1	whole chicken (3 to 4 pounds), cut up	3	large fresh parsley sprigs
2	large onions	1	parsnip, chopped
3	large carrots, chopped	1	teaspoon salt
2	celery ribs, chopped	½	teaspoon freshly ground black pepper
5	peppercorns	12	ounces wide or thin egg noodles
2	large fresh dill sprigs		

Place the chicken, 1 onion, 1 carrot, 1 celery rib, the peppercorns, dill, and parsley in a large stockpot. Cover with cold water. Bring to a boil over high heat. Reduce the heat to low, cover, and simmer for 4 hours. Cool slightly.

Place a sieve over a large bowl and strain the chicken and vegetables from the broth. Refrigerate the broth for 3 hours or overnight, or until congealed and the fat has risen to the top.

Meanwhile, remove the chicken from the bones and shred into bite-size pieces. Discard the chicken skin and bones, vegetables, peppercorns, dill, and parsley. Refrigerate the chicken.

When the broth is completely chilled, remove and discard the fat from the top of the broth. Chop the remaining onion, carrots, and celery rib.

In a large stockpot, combine the broth, chopped vegetables, parsnip, salt, and black pepper. Bring to a boil over high heat. Reduce the heat to low, cover, and simmer for 1 hour.

Meanwhile, cook the noodles according to package directions.

Add the noodles and chicken to the broth and simmer for 5 minutes, or until heated through.

Makes 6 servings

Per serving: 404 calories, 34 g protein, 53 g carbohydrates, 6 g fat, 133 mg cholesterol, 5 g fiber, 514 mg sodium

In the winter, the aroma of chicken soup simmering on the stove is as soothing as it gets. I love noodles in my soup, but 1½ cups cooked rice would work just as well for a change of pace.

KITCHEN TIPS

Chicken soup may be prepared many ways. Sometimes I like to keep the noodles separate from the broth, placing the cooked noodles into soup bowls and topping with the broth. If I don't want to use another pot, I will cook the noodles in the broth. This will thicken and cloud the soup a bit, but it is another delicious way to eat this classic soup.

If I am in a hurry but want some homemade soup, I will use boneless, skinless chicken breasts and prepared chicken broth, simmering it for about an hour with the chicken, seasonings, and vegetables.

PORT-BRAISED LAMB SHANKS

4	lamb shanks (about 3 pounds), cracked	2	whole garlic bulbs, cut into thick slices
½	teaspoon salt	1	teaspoon whole mustard seeds
½	teaspoon freshly ground black pepper	5	whole juniper berries (optional)
1	bottle (750 ml) ruby port	3	tablespoons butter
4	carrots, cut into 1" pieces	¼	cup chopped fresh mint
1	large onion, sliced		

Preheat the oven to 500°F. Place the lamb in a heavy roasting pan and sprinkle with ¼ teaspoon of the salt and ¼ teaspoon of the pepper. Roast for 20 minutes, or until browned.

Reduce the heat to 350°F.

Add the port, carrots, onion, garlic, mustard seeds, and juniper berries, if using. Roast for 1 hour, or until the lamb is very tender and nearly falling off the bone. Turn the shanks and baste with the sauce every 20 minutes.

Remove the lamb, carrots, and garlic to a large platter. Keep warm.

Strain the sauce through a cheesecloth-lined sieve into a small saucepan. Bring to a boil over high heat. Cook for 5 minutes, or until reduced by half. Whisk in the butter. Pour the sauce over the meat and carrots. Sprinkle with the mint.

If the sauce is too thin, pour it into a small saucepan and over medium heat, reduce it to the desired thickness.

Makes 4 servings

Per serving: 465 calories, 26 g protein, 27 g carbohydrates, 15 g fat, 99 mg cholesterol, 4 g fiber, 899 mg sodium

The pan juices of this turkey are delicious drizzled over the turkey meat. Continuous basting is the trick to creating great flavor and moistness in the breast.

SOY AND ORANGE–GLAZED TURKEY

2	large oranges, quartered	½	cup soy sauce or tamari
1	large leek, whites only, sliced	1	cup pure maple syrup or honey
6	whole star anise	½	cup orange juice
1	whole turkey (12 to 14 pounds)		

Preheat the oven to 325°F.

Place the oranges, leek, and star anise in the cavity of the turkey. Place the turkey, breast side up, on a rack in a large roasting pan.

In a medium saucepan over high heat, bring the soy sauce or tamari, maple syrup or honey, and orange juice to a boil. Continue boiling for 5 minutes, or until reduced by one-third.

Pour the soy mixture over the turkey, covering as much of the surface as possible. Roast for 3 to 3¾ hours, basting every 30 minutes, or until a thermometer inserted in a thigh registers 180°F. Let stand for 20 minutes before carving.

Use the pan juices as a sauce for the turkey.

Makes 12 servings

Per serving: 340 calories, 58 g protein, 10 g carbohydrates, 6 g fat, 130 mg cholesterol, 0 g fiber, 792 mg sodium

CHICKEN WITH DRIED CHERRIES, OLIVES, AND CHILES

1	teaspoon paprika	½	cup dried cherries
¼	teaspoon salt	½	cup kalamata olives, pitted
¼	teaspoon freshly ground black pepper	2	tablespoons honey
4	bone-in chicken breast halves, skinned	1	cinnamon stick, broken in half
2	tablespoons extra virgin olive oil	1	teaspoon ground cumin
1	small red onion, chopped	1–2	hot chile peppers (such as cayenne, red jalapeño, and habenero), halved, seeded, and minced
1½	cups chicken broth		

The combination of the rich sweetness of the cherries with the salty olives and spicy chiles may seem odd at first, but after one bite, this dish will become a regular because the flavors are so marvelous. I prefer using chicken breasts on the bone because they are much juicier; if you are in a crunch for time, however, use boneless ones.

Preheat the oven to 400°F.

In a small bowl, combine the paprika, salt, and black pepper. Place the chicken in a large, shallow roasting pan. Brush with 1 tablespoon of the oil and sprinkle with the paprika mixture.

Roast for 45 minutes, or until a thermometer inserted in the thickest portion registers 170°F and the juices run clear.

Meanwhile, heat the remaining 1 tablespoon oil in a medium saucepan over medium heat. Cook the onion for 5 minutes, or until soft. Add the broth, cherries, olives, honey, cinnamon stick, and cumin. Bring to a boil. Reduce the heat to medium-low and simmer for 20 minutes, or until the cherries are plump and the sauce has thickened. Stir in the chile pepper.

When the chicken is cooked, for extra flavor, if desired, drain off the pan juices and stir into the cherry sauce. Remove and discard the cinnamon stick before serving.

Place the chicken on a serving platter and top with the sauce.

Makes 4 servings

Per serving: 367 calories, 24 g protein, 44 g carbohydrates, 12 g fat, 54 mg cholesterol, 1 g fiber, 538 mg sodium

WINTER VEGETABLE PASTA WITH CHEESE

12 ounces angel hair or linguine pasta

3 tablespoons extra virgin olive oil

1 onion, peeled and cut into small wedges

2–3 garlic cloves, minced

2 tablespoons balsamic vinegar

½ cup chicken or vegetable broth

4 cups cooked winter vegetables (such as parsnips, rutabagas, winter squash, beets, broccoli, cauliflower, cabbage, and kale), cut into bite-size pieces

2 tablespoons chopped fresh oregano

3 tablespoons chopped fresh Italian parsley

Salt

Freshly ground black pepper

6 ounces cheese (such as feta, goat, Cheddar, or Monterey Jack), crumbled or shredded

¼ cup (1 ounce) grated Romano, Parmesan, or Asiago cheese

This is a great way to use leftover vegetables. Vary the vegetables and cheese for a completely different flavor combination.

Cook the pasta according to package directions. Drain and place in a large bowl.

Meanwhile, heat the oil in a large skillet over medium heat. Add the onion and cook for 4 minutes, or until almost soft. Add the garlic, vinegar, and broth.

Bring to a boil. Reduce the heat to low and simmer for 5 minutes. Add the cooked vegetables, oregano, and parsley and season with salt and pepper. Simmer for 3 minutes, or until heated through. Pour over the pasta, top with the cheeses, and toss to coat well.

Makes 4 servings

Per serving: 392 calories, 14 g protein, 47 g carbohydrates, 17 g fat, 92 mg cholesterol, 5 g fiber, 470 mg sodium

To make tofu attractive to both meat and non-meat eaters is always a challenge, but this sauce is a sure way to make that happen. Serve with your favorite coleslaw and squares of warm cornbread.

KITCHEN TIP

Chipotles are really spicy. Begin by using ½ tablespoon, and if you want it hotter, go for it!

TOFU WITH CHIPOTLE-ORANGE BARBECUE SAUCE

½	cup orange juice	2	garlic cloves, minced
4	tablespoons honey	1	teaspoon salt
2	tablespoons red wine vinegar	1	teaspoon ground cumin
2	tablespoons Dijon mustard	½	teaspoon ground cinnamon
1	tablespoon vegetable or light olive oil	2	pounds firm tofu, drained and cut into 8 slices
½–1	tablespoon pureed canned chipotle chile pepper (see tip)	2	tablespoons finely sliced green onions

In a 13" × 9" glass baking dish, combine the orange juice, honey, vinegar, mustard, oil, pepper, garlic, salt, cumin, and cinnamon. Add the tofu, cover, and marinate in the refrigerator, turning occasionally, for 1 to 3 hours.

Lightly oil the grill rack or broiler pan. Preheat the grill or broiler.

Place the tofu on the rack and grill or broil for 10 minutes, turning once, or until slightly blackened.

Place on a serving platter and top with the green onion.

Makes 4 servings

Per serving: 299 calories, 19 g protein, 29 g carbohydrates, 14 g fat, 0 mg cholesterol, 2 g fiber, 681 mg sodium

CREAMY CAULIFLOWER AND PENNE

1   cauliflower head, cut into florets

1   pound penne pasta

⅓   cup extra virgin olive oil

4   garlic cloves, thinly sliced

½   cup dry white wine

1½ tablespoons chopped fresh oregano

¼   cup kalamata olives, pitted and chopped

1   teaspoon crushed red-pepper flakes

4   fresh parsley sprigs, chopped

Salt

Freshly ground black pepper

¼   cup (1 ounce) shredded Asiago or Parmesan cheese

Bring a large pot of salted water to a boil over high heat. Add the cauliflower and cook for 5 minutes, or until tender. Remove with a slotted spoon to a medium bowl, reserving the water. Cook the pasta according to package directions in the reserved water. Drain and place in a large serving bowl.

Meanwhile, in a large skillet, heat the oil over medium-high heat. Add the garlic and cauliflower and cook for 5 minutes, stirring and breaking the cauliflower into bite-size pieces.

Add the wine, oregano, olives, and red-pepper flakes and cook for 3 minutes, or until the cauliflower is very tender. Add the parsley and season with the salt and black pepper. Pour over the pasta and toss to coat well. Top with the cheese.

Makes 6 servings

Per serving: 461 calories, 13 g protein, 64 g carbohydrates, 16 g fat, 0 mg cholesterol, 5 g fiber, 125 mg sodium

Cauliflower is a favorite of mine, and in this recipe, it takes the place of meat. I like cauliflower cooked all ways, but I am especially fond of it cooked as my mother did—until it is soft, creamy, and sweet.

KITCHEN TIP

For additional color, add a small can of drained chopped tomatoes to the skillet when you add the wine.

KITCHEN TIP

Any sweet citrus fruit will work well in this salad. Tangerines or oranges—especially blood oranges—are a good substitute for grapefruit.

PRAWN, GRAPEFRUIT, AND CAPER SALAD

3	red grapefruit		3	tablespoons walnut oil
3	cups water		2	tablespoons seasoned rice wine vinegar
1	bay leaf		1	teaspoon Dijon mustard
5	peppercorns		2	tablespoons chopped fresh mint
1	teaspoon paprika		1	tablespoon capers
1	pound prawns, peeled and deveined		1	bunch fresh spinach
1	small red onion, thinly sliced			

Halve one grapefruit. Squeeze the juice from one half into a medium bowl; set aside.

Cut the other half of the grapefruit into wedges. Place in a medium saucepan with the water, bay leaf, peppercorns, and paprika. Bring to a boil over high heat. Reduce the heat to medium-low and simmer for 3 minutes. Add the prawns and cook for 4 minutes, or until opaque. Remove the prawns with a slotted spoon and place in a bowl of ice. Refrigerate until ready to use. Discard the liquid.

To the bowl with the grapefruit juice, whisk in the onion, oil, vinegar, mustard, mint, and capers. Allow to stand for at least 10 minutes.

Meanwhile, over the bowl with the grapefruit juice mixture, cut the remaining 2 grapefruit into sections. Add the grapefruit sections to the bowl. Add the prawns, tossing to coat well.

Arrange the spinach on a large platter or 6 individual plates. Evenly divide the prawn mixture onto the spinach.

Makes 6 servings

Per serving: 182 calories, 15 g protein, 15 g carbohydrates, 8 g fat, 147 mg cholesterol, 5 g fiber, 234 mg sodium

MUSHROOM SALAD WITH LEMON AND OREGANO

¼	cup extra virgin olive oil	1	pound button mushrooms, stemmed and thinly sliced
¼	cup fresh lemon juice		Salt
2	green onions, minced		Freshly ground black pepper
2	garlic cloves, minced	1	head butter lettuce
1½	tablespoons chopped fresh oregano or 1½ teaspoons dried		
2	tablespoons chopped fresh parsley		

In a medium bowl, combine the oil, lemon juice, green onions, garlic, oregano, and parsley. Cover and refrigerate for at least 1 hour.

Just before serving, add the mushrooms to the bowl and toss to coat well. Season with salt and pepper to taste. Allow to stand at room temperature for 15 minutes before serving.

Arrange the lettuce leaves on a large serving platter or on 6 individual salad plates. Mound the mushrooms in the center.

Makes 6 servings

Per serving: 109 calories, 2 g protein, 6 g carbohydrates, 9 g fat, 0 mg cholesterol, 2 g fiber, 6 mg sodium

I always find it intriguing to take a regular ingredient, such as domestic button mushrooms, and transform it into something wonderful and seemingly exotic, like this salad.

KITCHEN TIP

For a lovely simple lunch, add 1 pound roasted chicken or seasoned tofu to the mushrooms before serving.

KITCHEN TIP

For a low-fat version, increase the flour to ¾ cup and use low-fat milk. For a luscious, decadent version, use half-and-half or heavy cream and omit the flour completely.

CELERY ROOT FENNEL GRATIN WITH GRUYÈRE CHEESE

1   large celery root (celeriac), about 1 pound, peeled and thinly sliced

2   russet potatoes, peeled and thinly sliced

2   fennel bulbs, thinly sliced

½   cup unbleached all-purpose flour

½   teaspoon salt

½   teaspoon freshly ground black pepper

1   quart milk

12   ounces Gruyère or Swiss cheese, shredded (3 cups)

Preheat the oven to 350°F. Lightly butter a 3-quart baking dish.

Place the celery root, potatoes, and fennel in a large bowl and toss well.

In a large measuring cup, combine the flour, salt, and pepper. Whisk in the milk.

Layer one-third of the vegetables in the prepared baking dish. Sprinkle with one-third of the cheese. Repeat layering, reserving the last third of the cheese.

Pour the milk mixture over all, pressing the vegetables to coat them. Sprinkle the remaining cheese on top. Bake for 1 hour, or until the vegetables are very tender.

Makes 8 servings

Per serving: 314 calories, 19 g protein, 20 g carbohydrates, 18 g fat, 63 mg cholesterol, 2 g fiber, 397 mg sodium

JICAMA AND BEET SALAD

2   beets, peeled and cut into matchsticks

2   avocados, peeled, pitted, and chopped

1   jicama, peeled and cut into matchsticks

12 radishes, very thinly sliced

3   tablespoons olive oil

3   tablespoons red wine vinegar

Juice of 1 lime

1   tablespoon sugar

2   tablespoons chopped fresh chives

½   teaspoon salt

Pinch of crushed red-pepper flakes (optional)

The complex fresh flavors of this crunchy salad are the perfect accompaniment to a bowl of hot soup served with fresh bread.

In a medium bowl, combine the beets, avocados, jicama, radishes, oil, vinegar, lime juice, sugar, chives, salt, and red-pepper flakes, if using; toss to coat well.

Makes 6 servings

Per serving: 228 calories, 3 g protein, 20 g carbohydrates, 17 g fat, 0 mg cholesterol, 9 g fiber, 229 mg sodium

SAFFRON COUSCOUS

2	cups vegetable or chicken broth	¼	teaspoon saffron threads, crumbled
½	cup raisins	2	cups couscous
2	tablespoons butter	½	cup pine nuts
½	teaspoon salt	4	green onions, thinly sliced

In a medium saucepan over high heat, bring the broth to a boil. Add the raisins, butter, salt, and saffron, stirring until the butter melts. Remove from the heat and stir in the couscous. Cover tightly and set aside for 5 minutes.

Meanwhile, place the pine nuts in a small heavy-bottom skillet over medium heat. Cook for 5 minutes, shaking the skillet often, or until lightly browned and toasted.

Fluff the couscous and stir in the pine nuts and green onions.

Makes 6 servings

Per serving: 403 calories, 15 g protein, 60 g carbohydrates, 14 g fat, 11 mg cholesterol, 4 g fiber, 468 mg sodium

In this couscous dish, the aromatic quality of the saffron blends beautifully with the raisins, especially when all three are finished with a drizzle of pan juices from whatever meat you might be cooking for dinner. It goes well with roasted leg of lamb or roasted chicken.

There are a handful of standard recipes that I have taught my children, knowing that no matter where or what situation, they can create from scratch something that will make people happy. I have yet to meet anyone who doesn't like warm biscuits. These drop biscuits are the easiest to prepare, with no need for kneading or rolling of the dough. My sons prepare them often.

(photograph on page 237)

ROSEMARY-LEMON BISCUITS

1	cup buttermilk	2	cups whole grain pastry flour
1	egg, beaten		
1	tablespoon lemon zest	1	tablespoon baking powder
2	teaspoons finely chopped fresh rosemary	1	teaspoon salt
		½	cup cold butter

Preheat the oven to 375°F. Line a baking sheet with parchment paper.

In a small bowl, combine the buttermilk, egg, lemon zest, and rosemary.

In a medium bowl, combine the flour, baking powder, and salt. Grate the butter into the mixture. Using your hands or a pastry blender, work the butter into the flour mixture until the pieces about the size of peas. Form a well in the center of the flour mixture and stir in the buttermilk mixture just until blended.

Drop the batter by large tablespoons onto the prepared baking sheet to form 12 biscuits. Bake for 12 to 15 minutes, or until golden and a wooden pick inserted in the center of a biscuit comes out clean.

Makes 12
Per serving: 173 calories, 4 g protein, 19 g carbohydrates, 9 g fat, 40 mg cholesterol, 1 g fiber, 404 mg sodium

POLENTA WITH THREE CHEESES AND MARINARA

5	cups water	⅓	cup (1½ ounces) grated Parmesan, Asiago, or Romano cheese
1½	cups coarse-ground polenta		
½	teaspoon salt	2	cups pasta sauce, heated
4	ounces smoked mozzarella cheese, shredded (½ cup)	2	tablespoons chopped fresh oregano
4	ounces provolone cheese, shredded (½ cup)	2	tablespoons chopped fresh parsley

In a medium saucepan over medium heat, bring the water to a boil. Gradually add the polenta and salt, stirring constantly. Cook, stirring often, for 30 minutes, or until the polenta thickens and is creamy.

Add the mozzarella and provolone, stirring until the cheese is melted and well-blended. Stir in ¼ cup of the grated cheese.

Evenly divide the polenta among 6 shallow bowls. Top with the pasta sauce and sprinkle with the oregano, parsley, and the remaining grated cheese.

Makes 6 servings

Per serving: 329 calories, 16 g protein, 33 g carbohydrates, 14 g fat, 35 mg cholesterol, 3 g fiber, 954 mg sodium

When I was a kid, my Nana made polenta a lot. She frequently served it with a creamy salt cod dish called baccalà. My brothers and I hated it (now I would kill for a bowl of her baccalà), so Nana topped the polenta with marinara, mozzarella, provolone, and grated Parmesan. It's real kids' food.

KITCHEN TIP

Be sure to watch the polenta and add more water if it seems to dry out too quickly. My grandmother used to cook polenta for hours, adding water when needed. Her polenta was the smoothest and most delicious I have ever eaten. Although we don't have the time that our grandmothers did to spend in the kitchen, be sure that your polenta is cooked to the consistency of porridge.

CHOCOLATE MERINGUES WITH FRUIT SAUCE

½ cup confectioners' sugar

2 tablespoons unsweetened cocoa powder

¼ teaspoon ground cinnamon

2 large egg whites, at room temperature

¼ cup whole natural almonds or hazelnuts

1½ cups orange juice

1 tablespoon honey

⅛ teaspoon freshly grated nutmeg

12 large dried apricot halves, cut into thin slices

Preheat the oven to 200°F. Line a large baking sheet with parchment paper.

In a small bowl, combine the confectioners' sugar, cocoa, and cinnamon.

Place the egg whites in a large bowl and, using an electric mixer on high speed, beat until soft peaks form. Reduce the speed to low and gradually add the sugar mixture, one-third at a time, beating for 3 minutes between additions, until stiff, glossy peaks form.

Spoon the mixture onto the prepared baking sheet, forming 6 ovals. Bake for 2 hours, or until the meringues are dry. If the meringues are not dry, turn off the oven and leave them in the oven for 1 hour. Cool on the baking sheet on a rack.

Meanwhile, place the nuts in a small skillet over medium heat. Cook, shaking the skillet often, for 5 minutes, or until lightly browned and toasted. Set aside to cool slightly, then chop.

Add the orange juice, honey, nutmeg, and apricots to the skillet. Bring to a boil over medium-high heat. Reduce the heat to low and simmer for 20 minutes, or until the apricots plump and the sauce reduces and thickens slightly.

To serve, spoon a generous amount of the apricot sauce onto 6 plates. Place a meringue on top of each and drizzle the remaining sauce over the meringues. Sprinkle with the nuts.

Makes 6

Per serving: 165 calories, 6 g protein, 24 g carbohydrates, 6 g fat, 0 mg cholesterol, 2 g fiber, 25 mg sodium

This beautiful dessert is a low-fat version of a fruit tart. I call for apricots, but use whatever dried fruit you would like. Dried apples, pears, or peaches work nicely. Or, why not use a mixture of several dried fruits?

Forget turning on the oven or dirtying a pot, and throw away that box of instant pudding. This delicate, moist custard can be prepared in 30 minutes. You need a flat steamer basket that is large enough to hold the ramekins. This is the kind of dessert that I sneak out of bed for and eat as a midnight snack by the light of the refrigerator.

STEAMED VANILLA CUSTARD WITH BANANAS

2	large eggs	2	bananas, sliced
1	cup whole milk		Sprinkle of ground cinnamon
½	cup sugar		
1	teaspoon vanilla extract		

Fill a large pot with 2" of water. Bring to a boil over high heat.

Meanwhile, in a medium bowl, whisk the eggs with the milk. Whisk in the sugar and vanilla extract.

Evenly divide the bananas among six 8-ounce oven-proof bowls or ramekins. Pour the custard evenly over the bananas. Sprinkle lightly with cinnamon. Cover each bowl with foil. Place in a steamer basket.

Remove the pot of boiling water from the heat and carefully place the steamer basket in the water. Return the pot to the heat and return to a boil. Reduce the heat to low, cover, and simmer for 25 minutes, or until a knife inserted in the center comes out clean.

Makes 6 servings
Per serving: 151 calories, 4 g protein, 27 g carbohydrates, 3 g fat, 76 mg cholesterol, 1 g fiber, 41 mg sodium

OAT BERRY CUSTARD WITH DRIED CHERRIES

4	cups water	1	cup milk
1	cup oat berries (groats)	⅓	cup sugar
½	teaspoon salt	½	teaspoon vanilla extract
⅓	cup dried cherries		Sprinkling of ground
¼	cup maple syrup		cinnamon
2	large eggs		

In a medium saucepan over medium heat, bring the water to a boil. Add the oat berries and salt. Reduce the heat to low, cover, and simmer, stirring occasionally, for 35 minutes, or until the liquid is absorbed. Remove from the heat and add the cherries and maple syrup. Keep covered and set aside to cool to room temperature.

Preheat the oven to 350°F. Place four 10-ounce oven-proof bowls or ramekins in a large, shallow baking dish.

In a medium bowl, whisk the eggs until light and creamy. Whisk in the milk, sugar, and vanilla extract.

Divide the oatmeal evenly among the prepared bowls or ramekins. Pour the custard evenly on top of each. Sprinkle each lightly with cinnamon. Pour cold water in the baking dish around the bowls to about 1½" from the bottom.

Bake for 30 to 40 minutes, or until a knife inserted in the center comes out clean.

Makes 4 servings

Per serving: 329 calories, 12 g protein, 55 g carbohydrates, 7 g fat, 115 mg cholesterol, 4 g fiber, 361 mg sodium

I love this nutty custard for breakfast or dessert. In winter, using dried fruit instead of out-of-season fresh is a good way to make use of organic seasonal ingredients.

KITCHEN TIP

Instead of cherries, use any small pieces of dried fruit, such as raisins or cranberries, or cut up pieces of dried apricots, dates, pears, figs, or prunes.

THE ORGANIC MARKETPLACE

AH! LASKA

P.O. Box 940
Homer, AK 99603
www.ahlaska.com

AH! LASKA provides certified organic food and beverage products. Their products are available in health food stores across the country, or you can check their Web site for on-line ordering.

Arrowhead Mills

P.O. Box 2059
Hereford, TX 79045

Part of the Hain Food Group Natural Food Division, Arrowhead Mills distributes organic food products through health and natural food stores. Products include all-natural whole grain cereals, beans, flours, baking mixes, and nut butters.

Barbara's Bakery

3900 Cypress Drive
Petaluma, CA 94954
www.barbarasbakery.com

This manufacturer produces all-natural cereals, cookies, crackers, and snack bars. Look for their products in natural food stores, or visit their Web site for retail locations.

Cal-Organic Farms

12000 Main Street
Lamont, CA 93241

Cal-Organic Farms is a certified producer of diversified organic vegetables. Their products are available in supermarkets and natural food stores across the country.

Cascadian Farm

719 Metcalf Street
Sedro-Woolley, WA 98284
www.cfarm.com

Cascadian Farms is a worldwide operation, growing, manufacturing, and distributing organic products primarily through select supermarkets and natural foods stores. Some of their offerings include potato products, frozen vegetables, fruits and juices, frozen entrées, and vegetarian entrées. With its own in-house agricultural department, Cascadian Farm is dedicated to agricultural research, and actively advises farmers on organic methods and practices. For more information on Cascadian Farm, see page 140.

Diamond Organics

P.O. Box 2159
Freedom, CA 95019
(888) ORGANIC
www.diamondorganics.com

This mail-order company harvests fresh produce the same day you place your order. Other offerings include organic breads and pastries, noodles and pastas, plus a unique selection of gifts. To receive a catalog, call their toll-free number or visit their Web site.

Earthbound Farm

1721 San Juan Highway
San Juan Bautista, CA 95045
www.ebfarm.com

Earthbound Farm distributes fresh organic salads, fruits, and vegetables, including salad kits with all-natural dressings and toppings. Their products are available in supermarkets across the country. Check their Web site for the store nearest you.

Eden Foods, Inc.

701 Tecumseh Road
Clinton, MI 49236
www.edenfoods.com

Eden, one of the largest natural food companies in the world, has been producing organic products for more than 30 years. Their offerings include organic pasta, canned beans, Japanese traditional pastas, sea vegetables, and organic soy products. Look for their products in natural health food stores and national supermarkets. For more information about Eden Foods, see page 18.

Fantastic Foods

1250 N. McDowell Blvd.
Petaluma, CA 94954
www.fantasticfoods.com

Fantastic Foods produces a large line of natural and convenient vegetarian foods, which include instant meal cups of soups, pastas, mashed potatoes, and cereals. To locate the retailer closest to you, connect to their store locator through their Web site.

Fetzer Vineyards

4040 Civic Center Drive, Suite 525
San Rafael, CA 94903-4191
www.fetzer.com

With more than 700 acres farmed organically, Fetzer is one of the largest growers of organic wine grapes in the world and is widely renowned for its organic grape growing process. You can find Fetzer wines across the United States in retail locations where alcoholic beverages are sold. Its other brand, Bonterra Vineyards, produces wines exclusively from organically grown grapes.

French Meadow Bakery

2610 Lyndale Ave. S.
Minneapolis, MN 55408
www.frenchmeadow.com

French Meadow, primarily a distributor, produces a variety of certified organic and yeast-free breads, bagels, and pizza crusts. They also have a line of wheat-free breads. Look for their products in supermarkets and natural food stores, or visit their Web site for mail-order instructions.

Frontier Natural Products Co-op

2990 Wilderness Place, Suite 200
Boulder, CO 80301
(800) 669-3275
www.frontierherb.com

Frontier distributes a line of certified organic herbs and spices, including black pepper, garlic, and cinnamon, as well as an assortment of organic coffees. Visit their Web site for a list of online stores or to send for a catalog.

Horizon Organic Dairy

P.O. Box 17577
Boulder, CO 80308-7577
(888) 494-3020
www.horizonorganic.com

Horizon, the leading organic dairy in the United States, has a large line of organic dairy products and juices produced with the highest regard for environmental and animal well-being. Product lines include milk and half-and-half, eggs, yogurt, sour cream, and orange juice, among others. Horizon organic products is the only dairy with products available in all 50 states. To find their products in your area, call their toll-free number or visit their Web site. For more information about Horizon Organic Dairy, see page 78.

Jamison Farm

171 Jamison Lane
Latrobe, PA 15650
(800) 237-5262
www.jamisonfarm.com

Jamison Farm raises free-range lamb without the use of chemicals, hormones, or antibiotics, and they supply lamb to the finest chefs and restaurants in the country. Orders are taken by phone or through the online electronic order form. They will also ship gifts, packaged with your personal message on a card and a booklet of recipes.

Lundberg Family Farms

5370 Church Street
P.O. Box 369
Richvale, CA 95974
www.lundberg.com

Lundberg Family Farms uses ecological farming techniques to cultivate whole grain brown rice, many varieties of which are organically grown. Their offerings include a large array of brown rice and specialty rice products. You can find their products in supermarkets and natural food stores or by visiting their Web site.

Mothers & Others

40 W. 20th Street, 9th Floor
New York, NY 10011
www.mothers.org

Mothers & Others is a national nonprofit educational organization. Its program and members have worked to further ecologically sound causes and practices, including the sale of organic foods in supermarkets. They believe it is everyone's right to know and choose how their food is grown and produced. Visit their Web site for membership and program information, newsletters, recipes, recommended reading, and valuable information on organics.

Muir Glen Organic Tomato Products

1250 North McDowell Blvd
Petaluma, CA 94954
(800) 888-7801, ext.1363

Muir Glen is the country's leading producer of organic tomatoes. Product lines include stewed and diced tomatoes, tomato paste, tomato sauce, pasta sauces, ketchup, barbecue sauces, and salsas, as well as no-salt-added varieties of some products. Look for Muir Glen tomato products in supermarkets and natural food stores.

Natural Choice

P.O. Box 1029
Oxnard, CA 93032
www.ncf-inc.com

Natural Choice distributes pure organic and vegan products, including soups and sorbets. Their products are available in natural and specialty food stores. To see if there's a retail location near you, visit their Web site.

Nature's Path
2220 Nature's Path Way
Blaine, WA 98230
www.naturespath.com

Nature's Path makes and distributes a line of certified organic breakfast cereals, breads, and waffles with all-natural ingredients and no artificial flavors or preservatives. To find Nature's Path products, visit their Web site to locate the store nearest you.

Newman's Own Organics
P.O. Box 2098
Aptos, CA 95003
www.newmansownorganics.com

Newman's Own Organics creates organic snack foods. Their first product, organic pretzels, are the best-selling organic pretzels in the natural food industry. Other organic products include chocolate bars, Fig Newmans, and Champion Chip Cookies. Check their Web site if you can't find Newman's Own Organics in your area natural food store.

The New Organics Company
639 Granite Street
Braintree, MA 02184
www.neworganics.com

The New Organics Company produces and distributes organic food products to retail stores. Product lines include breakfast foods like maple syrup, fruit conserves, and cereals; dinner items such as pastas, pasta sauces, and salad dressings; and snacks such as pretzels, tortilla chips, and salsas. To find New Organics foods, check their Web site for the store nearest you.

Organic Alliance
400 Selby Ave., Suite T
St. Paul, MN 55102
www.organic.org

Organic Alliance is a nonprofit organization that encourages environmentally responsible agriculture and promotes the benefits of organics to farmers, retailers, and consumers. Visit their Web site to learn more about organic foods.

The Organic Cow of Vermont
P.O. Box 55
Tunbridge, VT 05077
(800) 769-9693

The Organic Cow of Vermont produces a line of certified organic dairy products, among them milk, egg nog, half-and-half, and butter. Their products are available on the East Coast, from Maine to Florida, in health food stores, natural food stores, and many supermarkets.

Organic Trade Association
74 Fairview Street
Greenfield, MA 01301
www.ota.com

The Organic Trade Association (OTA) represents all facets of the organic industry in the United States, Canada, and Mexico. They promote organic products in the marketplace and guard the integrity of organic standards. The OTA is actively involved in regulatory and policy issues related to organic agricultural production. Visit their Web site to find a comprehensive listing of OTA members as well as information about publications, upcoming events, and many other topics.

Organic Valley
P.O. Box 159
LaFarge, WI 54639
www.organicvalley.com

Organic Valley, a co-op with some 200 member farmers in 11 states, uses healthy farming practices to produce certified organic vegetables, meats, poultry, and dairy products, including a wide variety of cheeses.

Pacific Foods of Oregon
19480 S.W. 97th Ave.
Tualatin, OR 97062
www.pacificfoods.com

Pacific Foods, an active supporter of organic farming, distributes a line of organic carrot juice blends as well as a selection of natural and organic soups, broths, and cream sauces. Visit their Web site for the store nearest you.

Pavich Family Farms
P.O. Box 10420
Terra Bella, CA 93270
888 PAVICH-1
www.pavich.com

Along with producing a wide variety of organically grown fruits and vegetables, Pavich Family Farms is the largest grower and shipper of certified organic table grapes in the world. Other products include organic nuts, raisins, dates, prunes, and other snacks and juices. Look for their products in supermarkets as well as in health and natural food stores, or visit their Web site for an online catalog.

Petaluma Poultry Processors
2700 Lakeville Highway
Petaluma, CA 94954
www.healthychickenchoices.com

Home of Rosie the Organic Chicken, Petaluma Poultry was one of the first companies to develop and market natural and free-range poultry products under USDA-approved labels. Their products are available through select retailers in the United States.

Rapunzel Pure Organics

P.O. Box 350
Kinderhook, NY 12106
(800) 207-2814
www.rapunzel.com

Europe's leading manufacturer of certified organic foods, Rapunzel's line of products includes items such as chocolate, whole cane sugar, Swiss chocolate bars, coffees, cocoa drink mixes, and soup broths. They have been a leading force in the trade of organic commodities internationally.

Rodale Institute

611 Siegfriedale Road
Kutztown, PA 19530-9749
www.rodaleinstitute.org

Founded by J. I. Rodale in 1947, this nonprofit organization is dedicated to working with people worldwide to achieve a regenerative food system that renews environmental and human health. Using education, communication, and research, the Rodale Institute shares information nationally and internationally with farmers, consumers, food industry leaders, policy makers, and children. For more information about the institute, visit their Web site or their experimental farm in Kutztown, Pennsylvania.

Seeds of Change

P.O. Box 15700
Santa Fe, NM 87506-5700
(888) 762-7333
www.seedsofchange.com

Seeds of Change is a mail-order company with more than 1,500 varieties of seeds, including heirloom and traditional varieties, vegetables, flowers, and herbs as well as perennials and bulbs (flowers, potatoes, and garlic). An excellent resource for Certified Organic seeds, plants, and foods, they also offer a selection of garden tools, books, and other cooking products. Their book, Gardening for the Future of the Earth, pulls together the best of sustainable agriculture practices, and their Web site contains a wealth of information, including a virtual farm tour. Look for their complete line in stores, or call or visit the Web site to request a catalog. For more information about Seeds of Change, see page 202.

Stone Free Farm

P.O. Box 1437
Watsonville, CA 95077

Stone Free Farm is a certified organic farm dedicated to flavor, freshness, quality, and working with heirloom seeds. On their 350 acres, they specialize in growing different salad blends, vegetables, herbs, and other specialty crops. Their products are shipped nationwide to distributors, wholesalers, restaurants, and markets.

Walnut Acres Organic Farms

Walnut Acres Road
Penns Creek, PA 17862
(800) 433-3998
www.walnutacres.com

The first manufacturer of organic products in the United States, Walnut Acres is the country's leading catalog for certified organic products and foods. Their product line includes peanut butter, soups, jams, hot cereals, and baking mixes. Visit their Web site, where they offer a full line of their organic products.

Westbrae Natural

255 W. Carob Street
Compton, CA 90220
www.westbrae.com

Westbrae distributes organic food products through health and natural food stores and some supermarkets. Products include Japanese products, condiments, soy and other nondairy beverages, and canned beans, soups, and vegetables, to name a few.

Whole Foods Market

601 North Lamar, Suite 300
Austin, TX 78703
www.wholefoods.com

Whole Foods Market is the largest retailer of natural foods in the world. Their extensive assortment of products includes lines from many organic growers and manufacturers. They operate in stores across the United States under the names Whole Foods Market, Bread & Circus, Fresh Fields, Merchant of Vino, and Wellspring Grocery. If you can't find a store near you, contact the corporate office or a regional office.

INDEX

Underscored page references indicate kitchen tips.
Boldfaced page references indicate photographs.

Conversion Chart

These equivalents have been slightly rounded to make measuring easier.

Volume Measurements

U.S.	Imperial	Metric
¼ tsp	–	1 ml
½ tsp	–	2 ml
1 tsp	–	5 ml
1 Tbsp	–	15 ml
2 Tbsp (1 oz)	1 fl oz	30 ml
¼ cup (2 oz)	2 fl oz	60 ml
⅓ cup (3 oz)	3 fl oz	80 ml
½ cup (4 oz)	4 fl oz	120 ml
⅔ cup (5 oz)	5 fl oz	160 ml
¾ cup (6 oz)	6 fl oz	180 ml
1 cup (8 oz)	8 fl oz	240 ml

Weight Measurements

U.S.	Metric
1 oz	30 g
2 oz	60 g
4 oz (¼ lb)	115 g
5 oz (⅓ lb)	145 g
6 oz	170 g
7 oz	200 g
8 oz (½ lb)	230 g
10 oz	285 g
12 oz (¾ lb)	340 g
14 oz	400 g
16 oz (1 lb)	455 g
2.2 lb	1 kg

Length Measurements

U.S.	Metric
¼"	0.6 cm
½"	1.25 cm
1"	2.5 cm
2"	5 cm
4"	11 cm
6"	15 cm
8"	20 cm
10"	25 cm
12" (1')	30 cm

Pan Sizes

U.S.	Metric
8" cake pan	20 × 4 cm sandwich or cake tin
9" cake pan	23 × 3.5 cm sandwich or cake tin
11" × 7" baking pan	28 × 18 cm baking tin
13" × 9" baking pan	32.5 × 23 cm baking tin
15" × 10" baking pan	38 × 25.5 cm baking tin (Swiss roll tin)
1½ qt baking dish	1.5 liter baking dish
2 qt baking dish	2 liter baking dish
2 qt rectangular baking dish	30 × 19 cm baking dish
9" pie plate	22 × 4 or 23 × 4 cm pie plate
7" or 8" springform pan	18 or 20 cm springform or loose-bottom cake tin
9" × 5" loaf pan	23 × 13 cm or 2 lb narrow loaf tin or pâté tin

Temperatures

Fahrenheit	Centigrade	Gas
140°	60°	–
160°	70°	–
180°	80°	–
225°	110°	–
250°	120°	½
300°	150°	2
325°	160°	3
350°	180°	4
375°	190°	5
400°	200°	6
450°	230°	8
500°	260°	–